Walk!

Devon

with

Kate and Alan Hobbs & David and Carol Hitt

DISCOVERY WALKING GUIDES LTD

Walk! Devon
First Edition - July 2007
Copyright © 2007

Published by
Discovery Walking Guides Ltd
10 Tennyson Close, Northampton NN5 7HJ,
England

Mapping supplied by **Global Mapping Limited**
(www.globalmapping.com)

This product includes mapping data licensed from **Ordnance Survey®** with the permission of the Controller of Her Majesty's Stationery Office. © Crown Copyright 2005. All rights reserved.
Licence Number 40044851

Photographs
All photographs in this book were taken by the authors apart from Flaming Barrel in Walk 14 provided by Ian Clifford .
Front Cover Photographs

Walk 13   **Walk 22**

Walk 8   **Walk 32**

ISBN 1-904946-36-4
(9781904946366)

Text and photographs © David and Carol Hitt & Kate and Alan Hobbs

Walk! Devon

CONTENTS

The Authors

As keen walkers, ex-engineer and teacher Alan and Kate Hobbs jumped at the opportunity of becoming researchers for DWG allowing them to ease their way into retirement with Walk Dartmoor! as the first challenge. During the project they confirmed their love affair with Dartmoor and have now finally managed to move to a smallholding on the edge of the moor where caring for chickens, sheep and a tractor compete equally with walking. Now being ideally placed to embark on the Walk Devon! book they eagerly joined forces with David and Carol to uncover some of Devon's hidden delights.

David and Carol were both born in Exeter and brought up with a love of the Devon coast and countryside; although their work took them abroad and to other parts of England they always vowed to return to their home county. Following busy business careers they now enjoy a more relaxed pace of life in a friendly mid-Devon village. After writing Walk! Exmoor they have thoroughly enjoyed exploring and rediscovering Devon's wonderful landscape; any spare time is taken up by attempting to tame their one-acre wilderness, otherwise known as the garden.

Acknowledgements

Catherine and David for their pertinent comments after "test driving" some routes.
Ros and David Brawn; alias Discovery Walking Guides, for their advice and professional support.
To friendly walkers we met en-route and other experts who shared enthusiasm and local knowledge.
The National Park Authorities, Forestry Commission, Devon County Council and other bodies for conserving and enhancing Devon's natural beauty, wildlife and cultural heritage.

Adventurous walking tastes are as varied as Devon's many landscapes and therein lies the appeal of this marvellous county. There's always something special to explore, whether you love spectacular coastlines, yearn to stride out across wild moors or stroll over tranquil hills and through pretty villages and valleys. Devon is a huge gem of a county, roughly diamond shaped, some 70 miles north south and 65 miles east west. It has two coastlines, the northern **Atlantic** and southern **English Channel** and three county boundaries, **Somerset** and **Dorset** to the east and **Cornwall** to the west.

And does our Devon diamond deliver walking experiences of the highest quality? Yes absolutely, as dazzling as the 108 carat Kohinoor and the rest of the Crown Jewels put together. Devon's amazing geological history has created a multi-faceted landscape ranging from rough uncut cliff faces to polished sun kissed sands, crystal clear waters and smooth rounded hills; even the luminous Devon air adds clarity and sparkle to the brilliance of the landscape.

A TOUR OF DEVON'S DELIGHTFUL LANDSCAPES

Steeperton Brook Walk 19

Right in the heart of Devon is **Dartmoor**, offering glorious views, wide-open spaces and an overwhelming sense of freedom. **Dartmoor** promises exhilaration, a great sense of wilderness adventure and a wonderful tranquillity of spirit; along with its rugged hilltops, spectacular gorges and idyllic river valleys there's history at every turn. Between **Dartmoor's** western fringe and **Cornwall**, the secluded **Tamar Valley** forms the county border; the meandering **River Tamar** with its tidal creeks and ancient quays was once an arterial highway for isolated settlements and thriving mineral mines.

The Valley of Rocks Walk 1

A softer landscape rolls across North Devon before ending in a rocky tour de force along the **Bristol Channel**. Sweeping vistas around **Barnstaple Bay** connect North Devon with **Exmoor's** southern ridge. There is wildness on **Exmoor's** desolate plateau and rugged cliffs, while cutting through them are winding valleys fringed with lime green beech hedges providing a more gentle landscape.

Mid Devon sits between the two moors, a quiet and peaceful farming area with hidden valleys amid pastures, river meadows and rolling rounded hills. Its relative flatness and broad panoramas allow huge skies to dominate. Small hamlets, church towers and village pubs are tucked away in a network of ancient bridleways, tracks and country paths linking small agricultural communities, cottage industries and family run businesses.

Hayes Barton Walk 16

The impressive escarpments of East Devon and the **Blackdown Hills** thrust strongly out of large open valleys dotted with picture-postcard villages and thatched cottages; big ridges abruptly end at the *Jurassic* Coast as vertical cliffs and small rivers run into **Lyme Bay** beside pebble beaches. After **Sidmouth** the landscape gradually softens into the heath land of **Woodbury Common** and the richer redder farmland of the **Culm**, **Exe** and **Creedy Valleys**.

Between southern **Dartmoor** and the **English Channel** lie the **South Hams** rich undulating pastures edged by the **English Riviera** coastline, a maritime fiesta for beach lovers and yachtsmen. Rivers flow between soft wooded slopes, gradually easing their way into the English Channel through flooded valleys and twisting estuaries flanked by high Devonian cliffs. There is an intimate feel to this whole area, a sense of being hidden away in a temperate climate with semi-tropical plants and pockets of hardy palms.

Devon's beautiful, diverse coast and countryside offers a splendid selection of walks for all ages and abilities. We crest each hilltop and headland with a thrill of anticipation wondering what new secret and delight will be revealed. Two questions arise, what caused this beauty and how has it remained unspoilt? The answers are a geological potpourri to the first and to the second, history, geography and a two big slices of luck.

A GEOLOGICAL POTPOURRI

If we think of the counties on either side as two slices of bread, then Devon is the sandwich filling, but not just boring jam, more like a perfect savoury combination of cheese, pickle, tomato, salad, rocket and a touch of home made mayonnaise. Unlike its neighbours the county has been blessed with an extremely varied geology, even giving its name to the Devonian period and examples of most geological eras are to be found. The earliest rocks dating from the Devonian period are nearly 400 million years old and lie as sandstone across the north and shale in the south. During the Carboniferous period marine trough activity resulted in various sedimentary layers being compressed into sandstones and mudstones including those that form the Culm Measures north and east of **Dartmoor**.

Volcanic activity resulted in **Dartmoor's** granite upland and earth movements created inclines and folds, seen today in Devon's rugged cliffs. During Permian and Triassic times the uplands were hot and arid while in the valleys, pebble and gravel beds were formed; marine deposits were laid when parts of Devon, particularly in the east were underwater. Earth movements also resulted in fault lines such as the Sticklepath fault running north from **Torbay** to **Bideford Bay**.

cliff formations at Warren Beach Walk 37

Since early man, fishing, livestock farming and a little arable farming supported the population. Mineral mining, cloth manufacture, shipbuilding and maritime trading formed the backbone of the economy and there is evidence of international trade over many centuries. During the 16th century wealthy merchants used waterpower to drive their mills and many prospered in centres such as **Exeter**, **Plymouth** and **Tiverton**; merchant adventurers including Raleigh and Drake set sail on trading expeditions from **Dartmouth** and **Bideford**.

Devon's first lucky break occurred during the 19th century industrial revolution when coal was needed to power large manufacturing processes; the county hardly has any of the black stuff and so didn't acquire large manufacturing centres with tall chimneys.

Geography played its part in a second revolution to bypass the county - the mid 20th century introduction of large-scale arable farming. With a hilly terrain and relatively poor soils it was not economically viable to create the large open fields needed for combine harvesters to operate profitably. So Devon still has its immense patchwork of small grassy fields, divided by banks and hedgerows and ideally suited for dairy farming and the rearing of high quality livestock.

DEVON TODAY

Inner Hope Walk 30

Tourism is a big employer with fine pubs and hotels increasingly able to deliver year round good quality food and accommodation. Devon's farming industry is at the forefront supplying locally grown meat and vegetables with 'low food miles' while fishing boats deliver freshly caught fish, crabs and lobsters. Although commerce and the service sectors have grown, the county is still a predominantly rural economy with relatively few large centres of population. Devon is fully participating in the 21st century technological revolution; the internet enables individuals to relocate while still effectively working in other parts of the UK.

Devon's landscape is carefully managed with over half of the countryside having protected status. Uniquely in the UK Devon offers: a World Heritage Site, two National Parks, a UNESCO Biosphere and five Areas of Outstanding Natural Beauty, all linked by 3,200 miles of footpaths.

With such a variety of landscape it simply depends on your taste but wherever you decide to roam Devon is geared up to welcome walkers all year round.

The coast

Coastal walkers have a wonderful choice, over 70 miles along the north coast and 120 miles along the **English Channel**. Both coastlines are part of the 630-mile South West Coast Path from **Minehead** to **Poole** and the Acorn marked trail is well signed and maintained. For rugged tramps along high cliffs the isolated and dramatic north coast is the place to head, while in the south, although the walking can be just as strenuous, it's broken up by sheltered sandy coves perfect for a siesta. Headlands make for invigorating walking with constantly changing views and a sensation of being surrounded by the sea, while in contrast, picturesque estuaries provide a safe haven ideal for relaxed strolls.

tramping down Wind Hill Walk1

looking down Chiselcombe Walk 1

The moors

Moorland walking is a different experience and we have included fine examples over wild terrain on both **Dartmoor** and **Exmoor**. **Dartmoor** can be challenging - it's remote, atmospheric and intriguing, yet also offers sheltered walking in beautiful valleys beside boisterous streams. **Exmoor** provides exhilarating hiking on paths and ancient byways over high moors and through steep sided *combes* and as a bonus also has a stunning coastline. These moorland walks are intended as tasters; there are two companion volumes in this series for **Dartmoor** and **Exmoor** which may tempt you to explore further.

The countryside

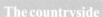
Little Dart River Walk 6

Determined to include a good countywide spread and varying landscapes we have discovered some lovely inland routes; take your pick from villages, escarpments, commons, woodlands and lakes. Some of our favourites are valley walks; we include three different **River Darts**: the **Little Dart**

Valley in mid Devon, a lovely tributary of the **River Exe** as well the famous **River Dart**. As countryside walking is normally easier underfoot you can cover a good distance but with all the twists and turns concentration is needed and GPS is surprisingly useful.

USING THIS BOOK

The walks are arranged in areas, starting from North Devon and going clockwise round the county. With adventurous walking in mind our distances vary from 5 to 12½ miles and wherever possible we offer a variety of scenery within a route. Many walks have short cuts and strolls within them so you can tailor the route on the day depending on mood and weather. Unless otherwise indicated, timings reflect our walking pace without stops, so we suggest you check your timings against ours early on in the route and adjust accordingly.

For something different why not try one of our five linear walks using public transport; as well as buses we also hop on trams, trains and ferries.

FLORA AND FAUNA

Devon is rich in flora and fauna. In springtime lanes, pathways and banks are

studded with primroses and orchids; woodland slopes are covered in drifts of gorgeous bluebells. A combination of undisturbed landscape and clean westerly air streams encourage the growth of many rare plant species, mosses, lichens and ferns; Sites of Special Scientific Interest protect unique and rare environments. Seabirds colonise the cliffs and opportunistic birds of prey catch the thermals during their waiting game.

The otter is currently regaining territory and salmon and seatrout do a good job keeping down the insect population on the rivers. Timid deer graze much of the countryside with majestic red deer inhabiting **Exmoor** and its fringes. Then of course there are the ponies on both **Dartmoor** and **Exmoor**, casually wandering across moor and road alike, always seemingly blissfully unaware of any traffic and just enjoying life.

A POSTSCRIPT

What actually kept us going during our research? Some mouth watering pub lunches and seriously addictive Devonshire cream teas were usually the reward for our efforts and occasionally if we timed it right, both!

Our two basic principles are :-

    i. **Be prepared** - always have with you the right clothing for the expected conditions bearing in mind the weather can change quickly particularly on the upland areas of Exmoor and Dartmoor and

    ii. **Be comfortable** - take only what is necessary for the walk.

Our 'equipment' list details the items that usually accompany us.

- A waterproof **backpack** (25-30 litre) big enough to hold spare clothing, food and drink with side pockets for the extras.
- Strong, waterproof **walking boots/shoes** that will give you support and a good grip on rocks and slippery slopes. Comfortable **socks** are a must and **gaiters** come in handy when tramping over the wetter areas.
- We find that clothing is best-worn in layers (with spare layers in a waterproof bag in the backpack). A **quick drying shirt/T-shirt** and a **fleece**, and **hat** and **gloves** in a side pocket. **Water and windproof jacket**, preferably breathable, is essential (a lighter one in summer) together with **waterproof trousers**.
- An adjustable **walking pole** for extra support and balance.
- A small kit with **plasters, bandage, small pack of tissues, sunscreen, fly repellent, bite soothing cream** and **antiseptic cream** and check for ticks on your return. **Money,** a **whistle** and **torch** can also be useful.
- Sufficient water, in 500ml bottles, considering the weather and route. We generally take a **packed lunch** (if we're not stopping at a pub en route) and survival rations for the remoter walks; **dried fruit and nuts.**
- Buy the best **guidebook** and best **map** (in a waterproof case) and carry them with you. There are hazards on some of the wilder walks and thus navigational tools are essential. A **compass** is useful for orientating yourself and for general directions, but a **GPS unit** is far more useful- see Using GPS in Devon
- Additional accessories **small camera, lightweight binoculars** and **mobile phone**.

Basic safety considerations
Before you set out:
- Check the weather - Weathercall 09014 722054.
- On Dartmoor check the firing times using freephone 0800 458 4868.

Let someone know your planned route and estimated return time.
- Unless you are an experienced walker don't venture into remote country
- Allow plenty of time and daylight to complete the walk. The timings given in this book are for guidance and are 'pure' walking times.

While you are out:
Know how to use your compass and GPS - essential for moorland walks
- Stay on route and if in doubt retrace your steps
- If the weather deteriorates consider your options; do not hesitate to turn back.
- On the coast keep to the paths and stay away from cliff edges
- Keep away from livestock
- In an **Emergency** phone 999 or 112 from a mobile phone or landline for Police/ Ambulance/Fire/Coastguard services.

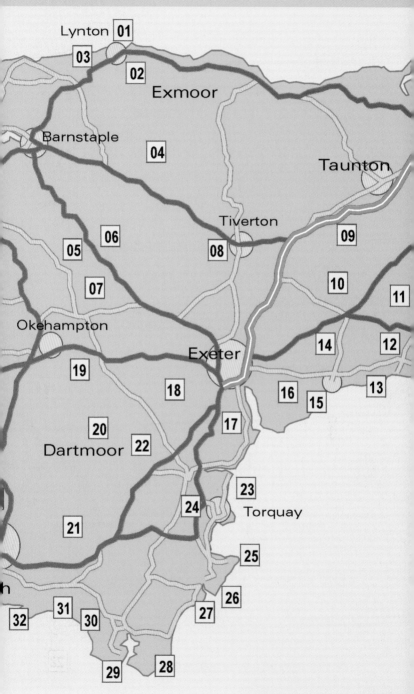

The GPS Waypoint Lists are as recorded while researching the detailed walk descriptions for this book. On the map section(s) for each walking route the Waypoint Symbols are numbered so that they can be directly identified with the walk description and Waypoint List for that walking route. All GPS Waypoints are subject to the accuracy of GPS units in the particular location of each waypoint. Where there is good GPS satellite reception, which is most of the time, then an accuracy of 5 metres can be expected.

Across the beautiful Devon landscapes GPS reception is generally excellent for the majority of routes. Occasional exceptions to 'excellent reception' may occur in steep valleys and woodland; these areas are identified as:-

Walk 1 Wps. 10-13 & 16-18, Walk 2 Wps. 5-8, Walk 3 Wps.4-5 & 16-17, Walk 12 Wps13-18, Walk 17 Wps 14-19 & 31-35, Walk 18 Wps. 1-3 & 23-25, Walk 20 Wps 2-4, Walk 25 Wps. 11-12, Walk 27 Wps. 7-10, Walk 33 Wps. 2-5.

GPS Waypoints are quoted for the OSGB (Ordnance Survey Great Britain) datum and BNG (British National Grid) coordinates, making them identical with the OS grid coordinates of the position they refer to.

To manually input the Waypoints into your GPS unit we suggest that you:

Switch on your GPS and select 'simulator/standby' mode. Check that your GPS is set to the OSGB datum and BNG 'location/position format'.

Input the GPS Waypoints into a 'route' with the same number as the walking route; then there will be no confusion as to which walking route it refers to.

Repeat the inputting of waypoints into 'routes' until you have covered all the routes you plan to walk, or until you have used up the memory capacity of your GPS.

Turn off your GPS. When you switch your GPS back on it should return to its normal navigation mode.

 our rating for effort/exertion:-
1 very easy **2** easy **3** average
4 energetic **5** strenuous

 approximate **time** to complete a walk (compare your times against ours early in a walk) - does not include stopping time

 approximate walking **distance** in miles and kilometres

 approximate **ascents/descents** in metres (N=negligible)

 circular route

 linear route

 figure of eight route

 risk of **vertigo**

 refreshments (may be at start or end of a route only)

Walk descriptions include:
timing in minutes, shown as (40M); compass directions, shown as (NW);
GPS waypoints, shown as (Wp.3).

Dubbed 'Little Switzerland' by the Romantic poets, **Lynton** and **Lynmouth** are surrounded by a landscape dominated by densely wooded river valleys, jagged rock formations and towering sea cliffs; this superb walk showcases some of the best of **Exmoor National Park**'s varied scenery.

The striking setting of the dry **Valley of Rocks** is our first 'wow' moment; to the seaward side a line of jagged peaks running to **Castle Rock**, while inland, gorse and bracken covered slopes mixed with grey rocks drop steeply from **Southcliffe**. A magnificent hilltop walk along **Myrtleberry Cleave** echoes the curves of the **East Lyn** before a descent to **Watersmeet**, one of the National Trusts most popular sylvan settings. A steady climb to **Countisbury** is rewarded with stunning coast views during our return to **Lynmouth** sea front where The Victorian Cliff Railway provides a relaxing way to complete our trek.

Access by bus: From **Barnstaple**, No 309 and 310. From **Ilfracombe** and **Minehead** No 300.
Access by car: Lynton (SS719495) lies just off the A39 on the B3234, 11 miles from both **Blackmoor Gate** and **Porlock**. Car parking in the town.

Shorter walk A: Walk through the **Valley of Rocks** to Wp.6 and turn left into **Lynton**. 2.1 miles/3.4km A140m/D140m
Shorter walk B: This walk misses out the **Valley of Rocks**. Facing the Town Hall go right along main street to Valley of Rocks Hotel and turn right down Queen Street, signed 'YHA via Sinai Street'. Climb to Wp.6 and turn left to join main walk. 7.1 miles/11.4km A465m/D465m

Facing the Swiss chalet-style Town Hall (Wp.1 0M) and taking a lane on the right hand side for 'Hollerday Hill' we soon leave the town behind, climbing through a small rocky canyon into woodland. Passing a turning circle we continue straight ahead ascending a 'Coastal path' to a kissing gate that opens onto a heather clad cliff side. To our right stands the distinctive snout of **Foreland Point** and on clear days there are views across the **Bristol Channel** to the **Brecon Beacons**; after a high level stroll, views open up along the coast to **Lee Bay** and **Woody Bay** and suddenly below us is the impressive rugged grandeur of the **Valley of Rocks**. Bearing left for 20 yards to a signpost (Wp.2 10M) we turn right down a steep shaly 'Valley of Rocks' path zigzagging to the floor; wild goats graze this area, nimbly prancing over the scree and so agile that they have learned to cross cattle grids, much to the chagrin of local gardeners. Turning right for 50 yards along a pavement to the edge of the

Valley of Rocks

cricket ground, we go left (Wp.3 18M) up a grassy 'Lynton footpath' steadily climbing into dappled shade between dry stone walls to a lane.

Bearing left downhill to a road junction (Wp.4 31M), we go right on a pavement beside dripping fuchsia hedges and soon turn left into 'Normans Cleave' (Wp.5 33M); this tarmac lane narrows into 'Alford Terrace' before dropping to a cross roads (Wp.6 37M). Going straight on for 'Lynbridge' overlooking **Lynton**'s higgledy-piggledy roof tops we continue down to a lane, keeping left to a T- junction in front of the **Bridge Inn** (Wp.7 46M). A 'Watersmeet' sign directs us down a slope to the right of the pub and left over a stone bridge spanning the **West Lyn**; swinging left for 'Watersmeet' into **Lyn Wood** we climb a well defined path through the valley. On clearing the trees there are fine Exmoor Heritage Coast views and a panorama extending to **Butter Hill** and **Countisbury Church**; on top of **Summer House Hill** we continue straight on at a path junction for 'Watersmeet' (Wp.8 64M).

Striding out beside field edges, the curving **East Lyn River** lies far below between densely wooded slopes and grey rocky outcrops; ignoring paths to either side we pick up signs for 'Hillsford Bridge' before twisting down over a stream and climbing past a stone seat to regain our hill top path. At the **Myrtleberry Cleave** post (Wp.9 95M) we join a blue tipped bridleway for 'Hillsford Bridge' and having descended between the grass mounds of an Iron Age enclosure, go through a gate down a track to a road. Bearing left a short way to a road junction and into the **Simonsbath** road, we cross the bridge ahead and immediately turn left through a gate onto a 'Rockford Bridleway' (Wp.10 108M).

This is easy woodland walking along a broad gravel path just above **Hoaroak Water** as it burbles round boulders and plunges into tiny pools before combining forces with the **East Lyn** at **Watersmeet**; there are times, however, when these spirited rivers become dangerous torrents, notably during the August 1952 **Lynmouth** flood disaster. At a path junction (Wp.11 121M) we go down the steps ahead, turning right and then left over a footbridge to the National Trust Information Point and delightful tea room at **Watersmeet House**. Our route goes left in front of the garden and a huge

Monterey Pine as we stay on the wider path to a junction beside the sweeping arch of **Chiselcombe Bridge** (Wp.12 126M). Going ahead on the 'Woodland Walk to Lynmouth' our undulating stony path starts near the river then follows a dry stone wall to a path junction at the foot of **Chiselcombe** (Wp.13 132M). (Here there's an option to continue along the valley to **Lynmouth**).

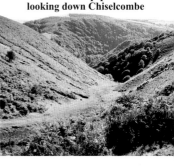
delightful Watersmeet

Taking a deep breath we go right on a 'Footpath for Countisbury', climbing steeply out of *sessile oak woods* on a grass path between bracken and *clitter* strewn hillsides; rapidly gaining height and cooled by welcome breezes we arrive at a sign post (144M) to the right of a circular stone and grass platform. To visit the **Exmoor Sandpiper Inn** take the 'Countisbury Off Road' path uphill for

looking down Chiselcombe

250 yards and return to this point. Going left across the grass rim we bear right beside a stone wall up a short path to the A39; turning left and taking care on this busy road we swing left at a **Countisbury Hill** road sign through a gate marked with an Access Land symbol (Wp.14 148M). A short climb on a grass track brings us to the ramparts of an ancient settlement atop **Wind Hill** and a path divide (Wp.15 152M) where we fork right on a 'Lynmouth Bridlepath'. From this

vantage point there are marvellous views across **Exmoor** and down the coast; a small structure in the **Bristol Channel** off **Foreland Point** is a hydroelectric generator utilising strong currents produced by the world's second highest tidal range.

Tramping steadily down a bracken slope brightly studded with clumps of gorse and heather we go straight on past a path junction to re-cross the A39 (Wp.16 166M); after turning left downhill walking beside the road on top of a bank, we bear right on the 'Coastpath' stepping down onto a winding path through woods to the seafront. A shelter on our left displays a mosaic depicting the bravery of the local lifeboat crew in effecting a heroic rescue in 1899. After a promenade through a pleasant park and across a white footbridge (Wp.17 180M) we turn right beside the harbour wall to the Rhenish Tower then swing left to an archway

tramping down Wind Hill

beside the Cliff Railway. The easier and sensible return to **Lynton** is on this smooth, eco friendly Victorian water powered conveyance (seasonal); walking purists can follow 'Lynton' signs, slogging up the steep hillside in long zigzags to North Walk, turning left to the main street (Wp.18 196M) and right to the Town Hall (198M).

Dry Bridge and **Shilstone Hill** lie at the end of a broad ridge running north from **Simonsbath** towards **Lynton**. Starting high on heather clad slopes there are wonderful **Exmoor** vistas during a descent into the delightful **Brendon Valley** and a pleasant riverside stroll including two charming hostelries. After a steady climb our gentle return is across the open moorland of **Brendon Common**, covered in a purple hue from mid-summer to early autumn.

A   GPS or compass should be carried in case of poor visibility.

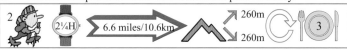

Access by car: is on the B3223 between **Simonsbath** and **Lynton**. 3 miles after **Simonsbath** we cross a cattle grid and the stone wall of **Dry Bridge** is 1½ miles across the moor. Parking area to the right. (SS 759455)

towards Shilstone Farm

Leaving **Dry Bridge**, a yellow tipped 'Shilstone' (Wp.1 0M) signpost points us north along a stony path between heather as we enjoy easy walking and fine **Exmoor** views. At a Trig Point (Wp.2 5M) there is a sweeping panorama over the broad valley to the smooth coastal ridge along the **Bristol Channel**; the A39 road runs just below the horizon and on a bright day the sun glints off matchbox sized cars. Our route straight ahead is marked with yellow topped posts as we gently descend, crossing over a rough earth depression heading towards a small belt of trees. In front of the field system we bear right, keeping parallel with a dry stone wall; our path drops more steeply as we descend beside a stream, bouncing along on springy turf towards Shilstone Farm tucked into the valley below.

Swinging right, then left over a stream we arrive in front of the farm where a 'Footpath' signpost (Wp.3 20M) points us between buildings and stables to a field gate beside Shilstone Cottage. Now, following the contour, we go straight across the middle of a sloping pasture and through a gap in a wall into the next field, bearing left downhill beside a hedgerow sprouting gnarled beeches. Climbing a stile we go left down Gratton Lane and as it starts to rise, dive right (Wp.4 27M) on a 'Rockford' footpath into a sylvan oasis. Steeply descending a delightful *combe*, our path stays above a stream jam packed with moss covered rocks; it's like a three dimensional jigsaw puzzle that doesn't quite fit together.

Near the foot of the *combe* a circular impound wall once provided waterpower for a large *overshot wheel* still standing against a wall; it operated a carpenter's workshop and there were many locations on **Exmoor** that made similar use of natural water resources. Keeping left of a galvanised roof we drop to a lane (Wp.5 34M) and turn left above the **East Lyn River** for a short stroll to the hamlet of **Rockford**, where refreshments are available at **The Rockford Inn**.

Our route turns right 100 yards before the pub across a footbridge onto National Trust land and under the oaks of **Wilsham Wood**, much of which is a Site of Special Scientific Interest. Going right for 'Brendon' (Wp.6 38M) our well maintained comfortable path winds above a sparkling river, its waters tumbling and foaming over jutting stone slabs. Shortly after Alderford Cottage, keeping left at a Y-fork (Wp.7 49M) through a gate, we continue on a path beside a field then along a riverside section of cobbled causeway. Strolling on a softer grass surface between stone buildings and railed paddocks we go along a track to a lane; bearing right to a road junction we turn right for **Brendon** over a bridge to a grass triangle. To visit the welcoming **Staghunters Inn** go right for 4 minutes and return to this point.

From the crossroads (Wp.8 62M) our route runs left along the **Malmsmead** lane; as we begin to climb the valley opens up with rounded slopes, rough

turning right for Brendon

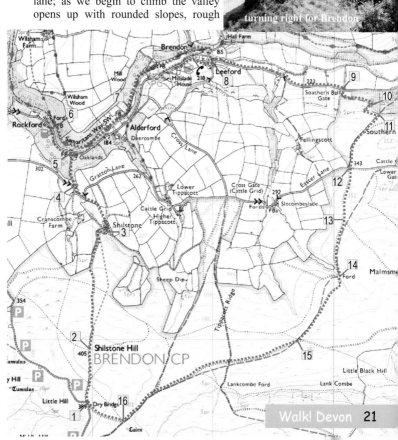

pastures on our side and a mix of gorse and heather on the far hill. After 14 minutes at a small green gap between the fields we turn right (Wp.9 76M) on a path for 'Malmsmead and Brendon Common', going through a gate and bearing left between encroaching bracken and a paddock. Steadily climbing,

views to County Gate

there are attractive views across to **County Gate** and down the length of the **Brendon Valley**. Entering a corner of **Southern Wood** we immediately swing sharp right out of the trees (Wp.10 82M) heading up a steep path on an open hillside; after gradually curving left for 3 minutes we arrive at an unmarked path crossroads and turn left on level grass to a path junction just above the wood (Wp.11 86M).

Now we strike right uphill on a broader path for 4 minutes until a large rutted track slants in from our left; bearing slightly right onto it, the gradient eases as we go through a gate onto a lane (Wp.12 94M). Pausing to soak up expansive views behind us we set off into the heart of the moor, crossing the road and going straight ahead on a wide

a shallow descent

stony 'Brendon Common' Bridleway. Forking right at an unsigned Y-junction (Wp.13 99M) on a grey coloured track a shallow descent past a few beech trees brings us over a ford; ignoring a right hand track (Wp.14 105M) we climb straight ahead for a minute then swing right up a stony rutted path onto level heather moorland. Encircled by a purple haze, sweeping views lead our eye down *combes* and over a green patchwork of fields to a backdrop of coastal hills.

At a junction (Wp.15 114M) we bear right on a well trodden track to a signpost marking our last mile straight on to 'Dry Bridge'; normally its easier under foot to keep on the right of the sunken track. A gradual ascent brings us level with a star sign marking a *cairn* to our left, and a large boulder set beside the right of our track (Wp.16 134M); turning right we stroll straight on along a broad path with views down **Farley Water** and across to **Cheriton Ridge** as we descend to **Dry Bridge** (Wp.17/Wp.1 138M).

3 The Heddon Valley, Parracombe & Highveer Point

For us this perfect day long North Devon walk provides a cracker of a route from the secluded wooded **Heddon Valley**, climbing through pastures to **Parracombe** before finishing with an easy (yes we did say easy!) cliff top saunter along a magnificent stretch of **Exmoor** coast. A gradual woodland and pastoral ascent during the outward half is matched by an equally comfortable return along an impressive 19th century carriageway offering stunning sea views.

En route there is plenty of interest in **Parracombe** village with its two parish churches, one a superb untouched Georgian gem. We may also catch sight of trains puffing along the narrow gauge line between Killington Lane and Woody Bay stations. There's a great short detour up to a coastal Roman Fortlet near **Martinhoe** before a sweeping grand finale into the **Heddon Valley**. GPS reception is intermittent along parts of the valley but the paths and tracks are clear.

4   3¼H   9.8 miles/15.7km   395m 395m   3

Shorter Walk: Turn right in front of **Hunter's Inn** up a steep winding lane to **Martinhoe**, going left at **Mannacott Lane Head** and on past the church to join the walk at Wp.14.
4.6 miles/7.4km A180m/D180m

Access by Bus: From **Barnstaple** and **Lynton** routes No 309 & No 310 to **Parracombe**. Start and finish walk by Post Office turning left at Wp.7.
Access by car: From A39 between **Parracombe** and **Lynton** signposted **Heddons Mouth** and **Hunter's Inn** (SS655482). Park on the road near **Hunter's Inn** or in National Trust car park beside shop and toilets.

Walking along the lane from the National Trust shop (Wp.1 0M) towards **Hunter's Inn** we keep left across a bridge, then turn immediately left through a gate marked 'Heddon Valley' (Wp.2 2M). Ascending a grassy path through deciduous woodland and soon high above the river, we go left at an unsigned path fork (Wp.3 8M); dropping downhill and ignoring steps to our left, we continue ahead, climbing a short flight of steps to a path junction. Turning left, our path descends through mature beeches beside a moss topped wall to a gate and footbridge; crossing over, we swing right through a field onto a lane at Mill Farm. Bearing right along the lane to a tarmac drive

beside 'moss topped' wall

leading to Heddon Valley Mill we go right for 'Parracombe' (Wp.4 25M); after 3 minutes a path detour takes us right over a stream beside rock pools and mini cascades before returning to the pine scented lane.

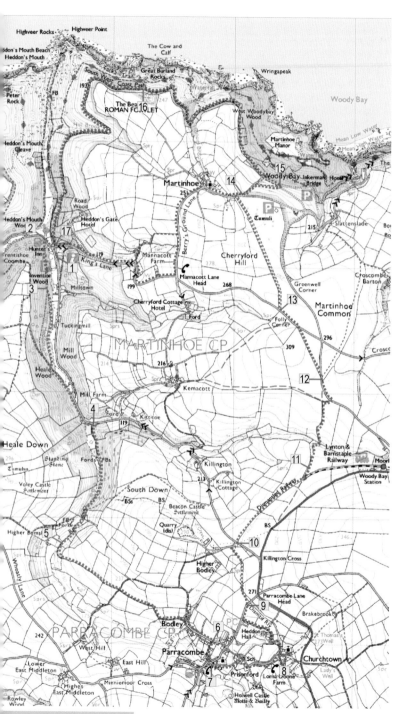

Just beyond a gate, bearing left for 'Parracombe', our gravel track soon becomes a grass path wending between bracken up a wooded valley to an unsigned path fork (Wp.5 40M). Forking left our stony path climbs out of the valley and through a gate; now guided by yellow way markings and 'Footpath' signs it's an easier ascent through rough pastures beside right hand hedges and tumbledown banks with an **Exmoor** panorama forming a backdrop behind medieval **Parracombe**. Going through a gate into an enclosed grass track, we head downhill between high hedges to the pretty hamlet of **Bodley**; the mound of **Holwell Castle**, a fine example of a *motte and bailey* fortification is clearly visible across the valley together with lines of *lynchets* in nearby fields. Strolling along a lane to the end of a lay-by, we turn right (Wp.6 64M) down a tarmac 'Public Footpath' between village houses into **Parracombe**; the **Fox and Goose** public house is down to our right.

Turning left for 40 yards to a road junction (Wp.7 67M) we go right up a lane past the 19th century Christ Church, built to replace St Petrock's Church. Bearing right for 'Church Town and Old Church', our lane climbs past the school to a bridge; although our route is left on a 'Bodley Footpath' (Wp.8 77M) it's definitely worth going ahead for a few yards to St Petrock's Church.

St Petrock's Church

Mentioned in the Domesday Book, regular services are no longer held in St Petrock's although it remains consecrated in the care of the Churches Conservation Trust. Its unspoilt Georgian interior, devoid of stained glass and other Victorian influence, retains a light airy feel. The congregation faced a splendid painted screen complete with royal coat of arms and biblical inscriptions whilst behind, a band of musicians sitting in raked pews provided accompaniment, evoking a time when sermons rebounded thunderously from a sounding board above the three-decker pulpit.

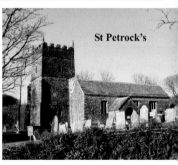

St Petrock's

Back at the bridge, dropping down a track between high primrose banks, we continue past Heddon Hall to a lane and turn right for 100 yards. Swinging left on a 'Higher Bodley footpath' (Wp.9 85M) yellow waymarks point us across a field along a low mound, once a railway bed. Crossing two stiles in quick succession we continue to a 'Footpath' sign; going through a gate on our left and keeping beside the right hedge we head along two fields and through gates onto a lane.

Turning right for 50 yards to a T-junction (Wp.10 95M) we cross over to Killington Lane railway station, a terminus on a restored section of the **Barnstaple** and **Lynton** narrow gauge line.

Keeping right along a blue signed 'Permitted bridleway' beside the railway there are coastal views to **Holdstone Hill**, **Trentishoe Down** and down the deep cut of the **Heddon Valley**. After going through a gate (Wp.11 106M) we keep left, hugging the edge of a gorse patch before curving left then right down a winding track to a gate and stream; crossing the stream and striking up the slope beside the hedge line to a hill top we bear right through a gate for 'Martinhoe Common'. Turning left along a lane and <u>ignoring a sign on our</u>

right for 'Croscombe Barton' (Wp.12 120M) we continue for 25 yards, then go left on 'Footpath to Folly Corner'; this sign can be partly obscured when the bank is covered in bracken. Entering a pasture and following the left hedge we crest the brow to be greeted with views of the **Bristol Channel** and a moorland landscape behind us towards **Woodbarrow**; it's a peaceful setting with big skies and buzzards wheeling overhead.

Negotiating a stile at the end of the field, we go left for a short distance on a lane; turn right into a field for 'Woody Bay' (Wp.13 129M); then it's on through another gate striding gently down the length of two long fields forming part of **Martinhoe Down** keeping parallel to the left hedge. Exiting over a stile and turning right along a lane for 40 yards we bear left across a small National Trust parking area (Wp.14 142M) and down a path for 'Woody Bay and Hunter's Inn'. Squeezing between heather and bracken covered banks we keep to the main earth path as far as the road edge and immediately turn left onto a track for 'Hunter's Inn' (Wp.15 147M). This broad carriageway engineered in the 19th century was used to transport visitors in horse drawn coaches along the coast from **Lynton** to **Hunter's Inn**; today it is a splendid hiking trail.

views back to Lee Bay

steep sided clitter slopes

Emerging from the trees and swinging seaward around Hollow Brook, mid summer swathes of lilac, plum and purple heathers cover the cliff side and rowan trees provide bright orange punches, but at any time of year there are glorious views ahead to **Highveer Point** and back towards **Lee Bay**. At a sign pointing left to a 'Roman Fortlet viewpoint' (Wp.16 171M) it's worth a short climb to appreciate the far reaching coastal and inland views the garrison would have had from this commanding but windswept position. Now putting our book away it's a pleasant downhill stroll into the **Heddon Valley**, swinging round Hill Brook before looking back down the steep sided *clitter* slopes to **Heddons Mouth**; continuing under an oak tree canopy we reach the road beside **Hunter's Inn** (Wp.17 198M) and go ahead to the car park (200M).

The unspoilt, imperceptibly changing landscape of **Molland Common** runs along a broad moorland ridge on the south west fringe of **Exmoor National Park**. Much of this Access Land is criss-crossed with small unsigned paths; how they continue to exist is a mystery to us as this area is so quiet and remote that we rarely see a soul - perhaps the ponies are trained to trot along them!

From **Anstey Gate** we cross the common to **Red Ford** then climb above **Danes Brook**, before dipping to **Lower Willingford Bridge** and a short valley stroll to **Upper Willingford**. Climbing past **White Post** we follow beech lined field boundaries to **Cussacombe Cross** and a glorious Devon panorama before descending to **Molland**. Our return through pastures via **Smallacombe** brings us back onto Access Land, dipping in and out of *combes* before a final climb to **Anstey Gate**. A GPS and compass are necessary in case of poor visibility across the common.

3/4 | 3½H | 9.2 miles/14.8km | 390m / 390m | 3

Shorter walk A: walk to Wp.9, turn left, following ridge road straight on past **Ridgway Cross** for 1¾ miles to car. 6.7 miles/10.8km A140m/D140m
Shorter walk B: From car park turn left, retracing ridge road for 1¾ miles to **Ridgway Cross**. Continue straight on for ¼ mile to cattle grid at **Cussacombe Gate** and turn left onto walk at Wp.9. 6.4 miles/10.3km A260m/D260m

Access by car: **Anstey Gate** is 21 miles from **Barnstaple**. A361 to **Haynes Cross**, left on B3227, following signs into **Molland**. Follow **Hawkridge** signs to **Ridgway Cross** and turn right signed **Dulverton** for 1¾ miles to **Anstey Gate**. Park beside the cattle grid (SS 835298).

From the cattle grid at **Anstey Gate** (Wp.1 0M) we take a 'Hawkridge footpath' down a lane towards Lyshwell Farm and after 2 minutes, level with the first gate on our right, (Wp.2 2M) turn left onto open moorland along a narrow stony unsigned path. The path immediately forks but rejoins after a few yards to become a rain trench; heading (NW) through a mixture of grass and heather our way becomes fainter, but continuing in the same direction we join a broader path slanting in from our left (Wp.3 8M). Bearing gently right on this wider route, we head down into the valley, aiming for the foot of an earth path going up the far hillside; Lyshwell

heading down into the valley

Farm's stark grey buildings appear to our right as we descend an eroded peaty path to a stream.
Splashing through **Red Ford** (Wp.4 17M) and swinging right between gorse we climb large stone steps and ignoring paths on either side, head straight on

uphill (ENE) to the brow and a gate in the hedge line. We turn left in front of the gate, strolling parallel to field boundaries until the wall turns sharp right downhill (Wp.5 34M); at this corner we leave the wall, bearing slightly left of a solitary hawthorn tree to pick up a contour path. Striding beside a bank along a shallow, bleak looking valley we are cheered by patches of purple heather during a gradual descent to **Lower Willingford Bridge** (Wp.6 54M)

Danes Brook

and a pretty resting place beside **Danes Brook**; the water course forms the boundary between Devon and Somerset.

Our way lies on up the narrowing valley but in front of us is a boggy patch, so crossing slightly left to a cattle grid sign we leave the road on a path, curving first to our left then bearing right to the foot of a bluff. The path runs along the valley floor beside a wire fence to a log and wire mesh interceptor slung across the stream. Our choice for the next ¼ mile depends on the depth of the stream; in fine weather when the water is low and it's easily fordable, we make our way along the right bank then splash back into Devon and up to **Upper Willingford Bridge** (Wp.7 66M). If the stream is too deep, we turn left up a steep slope, scrambling through bracken for 100 yards and turn right along a contour path to the bridge.

Bearing left from the gated bridge on a 'Bridleway to White Post' we wind up a grey gravel vehicle track across broad moorland to a field wall keeping left alongside it to **White Post** crossroads (Wp.8 81M) and a welcome bench. After a 5 minute stroll along the **Molland** road we bear right through heather to the corner of the hedge line about 50 yards away. Bearing left, we gradually climb a path beside the right hand hedge; in high summer nimble limbo dancing is needed to negotiate overhanging beech branches and in some parts it's easier to keep a little way out, parallel to the trees. Treading softly up this quiet section to the moorland crest we may be lucky to spot red deer, but are more likely to encounter **Exmoor** ponies before joining the road at **Cussacombe Gate.**

Going right beside the cattle grid (Wp.9 102M) and left on a blue marked 'Molland Bridleway' it's a comfortable grassy start before we continue along a stony path some 50 yards out from the left hedge, heading down to a gate beside a lane. The fine panorama contains many miles of hedgerows for which Devon is famed, stretching to

above the slopes of a deep coombe

Dartmoor's hilly skyline. Continuing for 'Molland' beside a left hedge to a field corner we jink left and right through a gate (Wp.10 120M), suddenly finding ourselves in a more intimate landscape above the slopes of a steep *combe*; below, a cluster of grey roof tops surround **Molland's** church. Strolling along the rim of the curving valley we arrive at a wooden latched gate opening into a sheltered track and descend to a lane (Wp.11 131M); turning left for 7 minutes to a T-junction and a grass triangle, we go left uphill for 'Hawkridge' to the Village Stores and **London Inn**. Note the two different signs depicting its history as a coaching inn.

St Mary's Church Molland

St Mary's Molland

St Mary's light Georgian interior, virtually untouched since 1740 has heavy uneven flagstones, enclosed high box pews and an impressive triple pulpit. There's a lovely story by Mark S Asher (www.exmoor.org.uk/molland) describing how the parish clerk was equipped with a stave with a wooden ball at one end and feathers at the other. Any man who deigned to fall asleep during a service would receive the wooden ball on his head. Sleeping ladies similarly would be tickled with the feathered end.

Turning left in front of the inn (Wp.12 140M) on a tarmac track, a 'Public Footpath' sign directs us past Bowchurch Farm and going diagonally right (NE) we follow waymark signs over two fields to a lane. Crossing over into a pasture, a footpath sign points us diagonally left towards the right hand end of a line of trees; going over the brow into a steep little *combe* we swing left down a broad grass path to the second 'Public Footpath' sign (Wp.13 153M). Turning right over two footbridges sandwiching a stile, we bear slightly left up the steep slope, climbing through a gate in a field corner, and stay beside a hedge, before curving gently right to a road. Our 'Bridleway' route for 'Smallacombe' lies directly opposite along a lane; dropping between banks filled with summer flowers and ignoring a right hand track we continue down past the farm to a gate opening onto Access Land.

Crossing a concrete bridge and fording **Triss Combe** we curve left up a track to a path junction (Wp.14 167M) where both Bridleway signs are for 'Anstey Gate'. Forking right, we swing up along the southern moorland edge beside dry walled fields; there are pleasant views up across **Gourt Mires** to the ridge and the pronounced defile of **Anstey's Combe**. Sauntering beside field

'to a path crossroads'

boundaries through a softer landscape our path alternates between grass and earth surfaces as we dip in and out of a small *combe* before dropping more steeply into **Anstey's Gully**. Climbing through a woodland fringe to a path crossroads, we go straight on signed 'West Anstey' and after 120 yards turn left at the first track junction (Wp.15 197M), then curve right towards a line of trees, making our way up the hillside to the car park (Wp.16/Wp.1 208M).

5 An Eggesford Woodland Trail

During this sylvan hike through the lovely **Taw Valley** we visit seven coniferous and broadleaved woods managed by the Forestry Commission, all set in peaceful surroundings and connected by quiet field paths and tracks offering beautiful views. Part of our route follows the otter paw mark symbols of northern Devon's long distance Tarka Trail, a 180 mile figure of eight, passing through countryside glowingly described by Henry Williamson in his novel Tarka the Otter.

Having cultivated woodland in this area for nearly 100 years the Forestry Commission now also undertakes conservation work and supports recreational activities on their Access Land. The first ever Forestry Commission tree was planted in **Flashdown Wood** in 1919; other plaques commemorate anniversary plantings, including the granite Queens Stone on the edge of **Hilltown Wood**.

Access by train: From **Barnstaple** and **Exeter** to **Eggesford** Station. Cross river up lane to **Cott Cross**, start and finish walk at Wp.19.
Access by car: **Eggesford** Forest is 22 miles from **Exeter** on the A377 **Barnstaple** road. Parking is available on the right in **Hilltown Wood** (SS 694105).

Shorter walk: Turn right at Wp.4 following Tarka Trail public footpath signs along a meadow and up a track to Trenchard Farm. Turn right along a lane to the War Memorial at **Eggesford** Fourways and then right on the Tarka Trail through fields down to Wp.20, near **Eggesford** Church. Turn right for 'Eggesford Forest'. 4.6 miles A150m/D150m.
Strolls: Colour coded trails are shown on information boards in **Hilltown Wood**.

From an impressive direction post in **Hilltown Wood** (Wp.1 0M) we follow the 'Forest Walks', bearing right past a barrier onto a level track and curving gradually left up a valley under a canopy of huge Douglas Firs. The Forestry Commission are retaining specimen trees hoping they will drop seed and regenerate naturally. After 10 minutes the track bends right over a stream and starts back down the other side of the valley; 60 yards after crossing the stream we look for a narrow unsigned path on our left (Wp.2 11M) and swing acutely back up through the trees, climbing to the woodland edge. Bearing left for a few paces to a field, we turn right on a path beside a hedge (Wp.3 17M) and with lovely views across the valley descend the Bridleway to a track junction; just above a road we turn right and carefully cross the busy A377 at **Chenson**.

an impressive direction post

Following a track beside cottages, we go over the railway line and **River Taw** to a signpost beside a gate (Wp.4 31M), marking

Wiseland Wood

the start of the short walk.

Continuing straight on along a 'Tarka Trail Bridleway' into conifers, we bear right on a wide track lined with foxgloves, climbing through broadleaved **Wiseland Wood** before descending to a gate below Hawkridge Farm (Wp.5 42M). Going right we swing up through the gated farmyard to a road and go ahead down the 'Coldridge' lane to a left hand bend; entering a field (Wp.6 47M) our 'Tarka Trail footpath' keeps beside the left hedge until a yellow arrow switches us into another field to a stile. Bearing right past a small ruin we enter **Burrowcleave Wood** through a pedestrian gate (Wp.7 54M) joining a pleasant path curving along the valley slope near the tree line. Sauntering through bracken clearings we cross a small stream, bearing left along the edge of **Great Wood** before climbing a short way and exiting over a stile into a large pasture. With ruined farm buildings on our right we bear gradually left to a

bracken clearings

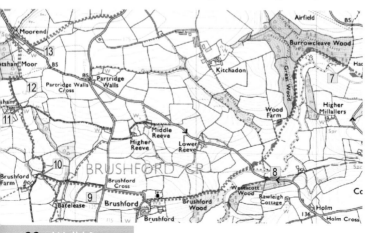

protruding hedge corner, then continue diagonally left to the middle of the far hedgerow where a hidden wire mesh pedestrian gate opens onto a footbridge (Wp.8 73M).

Now it's straight across the next field and over a lane onto a yellow marked footpath, crossing two fields and a footbridge; where the **River Taw** swings left we continue across pasture to a marker post in front of the wood. Bearing right, then left, we wriggle through rough grass and over a stile, climbing straight uphill beside the left hedge; behind us rolling pastoral views open up along the valley. Nearing **Brushford Church**, the track becomes a lane and after bearing right at a T-junction we swing left along a crest to **Brushford Cross** (Wp.9 95M), then go ahead on a blue marked 'Public Bridleway'. Our route descends between high hedges, across a stream and up a track; just before it bends left we turn right uphill through a yellow marked gate (Wp.10 102M), climbing beside the hedge at first and then swinging gradually left across the field corner to kissing gate. From here, it's a steady ascent up a long field to a gate in the top right corner; looking back, there are terrific views stretching across hills and valleys to Dartmoor.

pastoral views open up

Keeping straight ahead on a 'Public Footpath' (Wp.11 113M) between outbuildings, we bend right through a gate then left for 200 yards to the end of a shady *green lane*; going through a gate, we turn immediately right along an overgrown grassy track into a rough patch of land. A green 'Public footpath' sign (Wp.12 119M) points 90 degrees left, but there is no clear path and our actual direction is more like 45 degrees left.

Trudging downhill between waist high clumps of reeds and tussocky grass, keeping a copse on our right, we aim for an electricity pole ahead displaying reassuring footpath markers, then continue over a stile and footbridge in the bottom right corner. The garden glimpsed to the right of our short woodland path has several large ponds and boardwalks and was once a specialist nursery.

Our route turns right up a lane (for the **Lymington Arms**, go left for 5 minutes and return to this point) to the Old Forge house; turning left at a signpost (Wp.13 131M) through a gate and bearing left a few paces through a gap in the trees, we go right along a field path beside the hedge to a stile. In the next field our meandering path finally heads down to a gate on the far left; yellow arrows point us slightly right over a rise and through gates onto a lane where we are greeted with extensive views of both **Dartmoor** and **Exmoor**.

Turning left, a 9 minute lane stroll brings us to a 'Public Footpath' beside a pedestrian gate on our left (Wp.14 149M); going diagonally left across a field into **Haynes Valley Plantation** we stay beside the woodland edge, dropping to a gate on our left (Wp.15 155M). We turn right down an unsigned forest path for 2 minutes into a large clearing; keeping ahead along the right edge and slipping beneath low branches, we continue down a path to a junction with a wide gravel track. Going straight on to a large clearing and a Y-fork (Wp.16 166M) we bear left down through a gate and with a stream on our right, go along the foot of a field into **Stone Wood,** continuing to a blue tipped 'Bridleway Sign' (Wp.17 174M). Climbing left up a steep path into **Flashdown Plantation**, we reach a turning circle with wooden perimeter posts (Wp.18 181M) and go right along an unsigned track past an avenue of commemorative copper beeches and the first trees planted by the Forestry Commission.

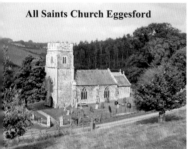

All Saints Church Eggesford

ramrod Douglas firs

Turning right onto a road and taking care down to a T-junction at **Cott Cross** (Wp.19 194M), we go right for 100 yards then left along a lane to the picturesque setting of All Saints Church, **Eggesford**. The church dates from the 14th century and contains several splendid monuments to local families and benefactors. Continuing to a Y-junction (Wp.20 202M) we bear left on a track for 'Eggesford Forest' then, following footpath markers, descend a path across a railway bridge over the **Taw**; shortly after, going left under the Tarka line we swing left on a field path to an animal pen and stile. Carefully crossing the A377 we go up a footpath and turn right behind a cottage enjoying a final stroll beside ramrod Douglas Firs along the track leading to the car park (219M).

rural tranquillity

Hidden in deepest Devon, **Chulmleigh** parish has a rare accolade from the Campaign for the Protection of Rural England as an area of rural tranquillity; this includes the picturesque **Little Dart River** flowing beside meadows and rounded wooded hills between the farming communities of **Chawleigh** and **Chulmleigh**. Our route from **Chawleigh** visits **West Burridge ancient settlement**, crosses the river at **Cheldon Bridge** and heads downstream to the small historic hilltop town of **Chulmleigh**; we return along a valley bridle way before a final woodland climb to **Chawleigh**.

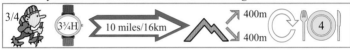

3/4   3¾H   10 miles/16km   400m   400m   4

Access by bus: No 377 **Exeter**, **Chawleigh**, **Chulmleigh**,
Access by car: **Chawleigh** is 21 miles from Exeter. Take A377 and turn right at **Eggesford** station. Park in front of Church. (SS712126)

Shorter walk A: Follow walk to **Cheldon Bridge** and **Stone Mill Cross** Wp.9, then left up a lane to **Chawleigh** 4.9 miles/7.9km A180m/D180m
Shorter walk B: From **Chawleigh** turn left downhill to **Stone Mill Cross**, turning left onto the main walk at Wp.9 6.3 miles/10.1km A300m/D300m

Starting from **Chawleigh** with the Church lych gate (Wp.1 0M)) behind us, we set off alongside a stone wall crossing a road junction onto a 'Public Footpath' gravel track leading to a stile and gate. Keeping ahead beside a hedge we drop down into trees, step over a stream and stile, then following yellow waymarkings go right and immediately bear left (WP.2 8M) climbing through gorse and bracken to a field. The waymark points too far left, so we go straight ahead climbing to the right of an electricity pole to a gate.

Striding along a broad ridge track between fields we pass a house guarded by yappy dogs, cross a lane (Wp.3 22M) and go along a grass 'Footpath' between hedgerows; entering a rough patch of brambles our path curves left to a gate with fancy ironwork. Bearing half right through a pasture and staying to the right of a large tree, we cross to a gate in the opposite hedgerow; now with pastoral views on either side, we continue in the same direction over three fields, then bear right on a short stretch of track to a lane. Turning left past the first farm buildings, we swing right through a gate (Wp.4 36M) onto a 'Public footpath'; our pretty, secluded grass track gently descends into a bluebell wood and bears right across a stream (Wp.5 44M). This wooded section can be quite wet underfoot, so after squelching our way through the muddy bits and shaking off our boots it's a relief to climb a broad track out of the trees and across a field to a lane (Wp.6 49M).

Our route turns left, but a short diversion ahead brings us to the ancient settlement of **West Burridge** where a large grass circle can be seen ringed with double banks and a ditch. Retracing our steps to Wp.6 (59M) we go down the lane through mixed woodland into the **Little Dart Valley** and over **Cheldon Bridge**; just beyond, a sign points us left 'Towards

Chawleigh'(Wp.7 66M) through scrubland. Crossing a stile we go along a large river meadow, gradually climbing a slope and keeping slightly to the right of the large trees before dipping down over a streamlet to a gap in the hedge ahead. Strolling down a long pasture we cross a stile into woodland following a stony path along the river bank for a short while before entering another long meadow, gradually curving left to **Leigh Bridge** (Wp.8 88M).

Turning right along a lane we pass a junction en route to **Stone Mill Cross** (Wp.9 94M) where shorter walk A returns up the 'Chawleigh' lane. Going straight on for 'Gidley Arms' to a sharp bend (Wp.10 99M), we continue ahead on a concrete track; beyond Stone Edge the track becomes a blue marked 'Public Bridleway' as we climb a slope above the broadening valley towards Stone Barton Farm. Just before the farm we bear left on a tarmac drive (Wp.11 109M) then left again beside a stone wall to a large cattle shed; a blue arrow beside the light switch points us left around the side of the building. Going left down a 'Public Bridleway' beside a woodland edge we pass through gates and over a footbridge into a field; going straight across into a hedgerow lined track (Wp.12 126M) a steady ascent beside a brook brings us to a concrete lane, then it's on up the track, which in wet weather doubles up as a stream.

Crossing a lane we pause beside a stile (Wp.13 141M) to take in the pleasant view over the valley to **Chulmleigh**. A yellow 'Footpath' arrow points gradually left down a steep slope to the bottom left corner of the field; skirting a short section of fencing we drop down a narrow path surrounded by gorse and bracken to the foot of the hill and through a gate onto a lane (Wp.14

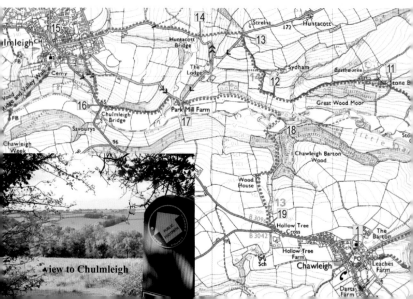

view to Chulmleigh

148M). Turning right it's a steady climb into **Chulmleigh** and along a cottage-lined street with thatched eyebrow porches to Red Lion corner (Wp.15 165M).

Turning left to a blue parish pump and keeping left of the substantial Old Rectory gates along a side road, we turn right just beyond Davy Park down a very steep lane past the pink cob walls of Egypt cottage, one of **Chulmleigh's** oldest houses. Egypt Lane was once a main route into the town but heavy horse drawn coaches couldn't negotiate it, so a new road with a shallower gradient was cut up **Chulmleigh Hill**. Turning left down the 'new road' for 100 yards we bear left through a gate (Wp.16 174M) along a 'Public Bridleway' on a tree enclosed level track; the *leat* beside us was used to power several mills including one that generated sufficient electricity for the town. Heading on through fields, we turn right along a lane for a short distance then climb a stile (Wp.17 184M) beside Park Mill onto a 'Public footpath'; hugging the hedge line as far as a stile we cross the leat on footbridges and bear left parallel to a hedge across large meadows to a footbridge over the **Little Dart** (Wp.18 195M).

Stooping through a small coniferous tunnel we are guided by yellow marker posts, bearing half right on a grass path, then left, right, left, onto a dirt track. Climbing out of the wood we turn right through the first opening and across a field to the far hedge; our route goes left beside the hedge to a gap then across another field to a road (Wp.19 209M). Going left and straight on at **Hollow Tree Cross** we follow the 'Chawleigh' road past the **Royal Oak** pub then turn left over a metal stile along a 'Footpath' through the recreation field to the Church (Wp.20/Wp.1 218M).

Historic Chulmleigh

The Saxon settlement of **Chulmleigh** was on the main road from **Exeter** to **Barnstaple** until a 19th century turnpike was built along the **Taw Valley**. The town was granted a charter in 1253 for a fair and market and this tradition still continues at the end of July. The church of **St Mary Magdalene** has some fine features including a 15th century Rood screen. **The Old Court House** dating back to 1633 is a friendly country inn; in the past it welcomed Charles 1 during his first royal tour of the West Country. In a bedroom above the bar that was once part of the court room, is a re-gilded original Stuart coat of arms and frieze.

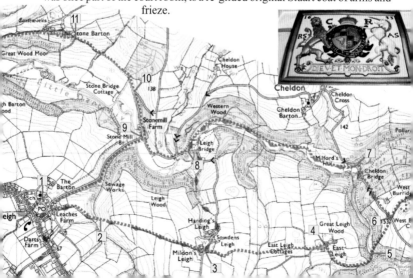

If our walks were in alphabetical order this would be the last entry, but it's first in our list of Mid Devon village walks. The manor of **Zeal Monachorum** was gifted by King Canute to Buckfast Abbey in 1016 and the village clusters round the Church of **St Peter the Apostle**; in the churchyard is a splendid veteran yew tree with a girth of more than 17 feet. The village stands above two small rivers in an attractive landscape of hilly pastures and valley meadows studded with woods and copses; springtime hedges and banks are liberally sprinkled with primroses, violets and orchids while woods are carpeted with daffodils and bluebells.

Part of our walk along the hillsides and peaceful valleys of the **Rivers Yeo** and **Gissage** follows the 45 mile **Devonshire Heartland Way**; its white logo depicts the Spindle Berry Flower. We start and end at the popular **Waie Inn**, a pub and leisure complex on the village edge; not your typical village inn, but very welcoming and open all day.

Access by car: From **Crediton** take A377 to **Copplestone** and A3072 for 3½ miles to **Bow**. Turn right for 2 miles to **Zeal Monachorum** and first right in village. Park at side of broad road before **Waie Inn**.

Shorter walk A: Follow walk to Wp.9, turn left to church and right downhill, back to the **Waie Inn**. 3 miles/4.8km A160m/D160m
Shorter walk B: Follow walk directions to junction by church and turn right along road. Follow remainder of walk from Wp.10. 3.2 miles/5.1km A115m/D115m

St Peter the Apostle Church

a delightful hidden spot

With our back to the **Waie Inn** sign (SS 721038) (Wp.1 0M) we go up a lane to a T-junction, bearing right and climbing steeply between cottages to the village junction beside the church; going left signed 'Bondleigh' for 40 yards, we turn right up a lane (Wp.2 6M) for 'East Foldhay'. From the crest there are wide undulating views across a patchwork of fields to the villages of **Lapford** and **Morchard Bishop** which continue as we descend to a gate and 'Public Footpath' sign on our left (Wp.3 12M). Dropping beside a right hedge filled with spring flowers, we cross a stile into a daffodil and bluebell wood, rejoining the lane in front of a gate (Wp.4 16M). However, before going through, there is a delightful hidden spot 20 yards along the stream bank with a bench and arched footbridge.

Entering East Foldhay gate on a gravel track along the valley floor, we go between farm buildings housing a 4x4 off-road centre, then after two gates swing right through a pedestrian gate (Wp.5 23M) into a field; from here yellow footpath arrows will guide us back to the village. Climbing to a point where the hedge sticks out, we strike left across a pasture into the next field, striding along a verge to a path intersection in the top left corner (Wp.6 31M). Turning left into a grass track and gently dropping between banks of springtime primroses we go through a gate and around Great Foldhay Farm on a concrete track; swinging away from the house for 20 yards we turn left through a gate (Wp.7 36M) and diagonally right into the valley. Going over a stile and concrete plank we arrive

between banks of
springtime primroses

at a wooden footbridge that crosses **Gissage Lake**; in this instance Lake means a small river.

Turning right through a gate into a long rough pasture past a bed of reeds, we gradually curve left, heading through a large gap ahead and on in the same direction, gently climbing to a gate. As buzzards glide overhead, we climb the slope in front dipping in and out of a large depression before crossing a stile in the far hedge. The lovely view back along the quiet valley isn't completely timeless, as what look like medieval cultivation strips on the far hillside, are in fact tracks of the 4 x 4 off-road centre. Bearing gently right up hill through a gate set in a fence line we continue up to a gap in the hedge where a field gate

creating our own path
(see next page)

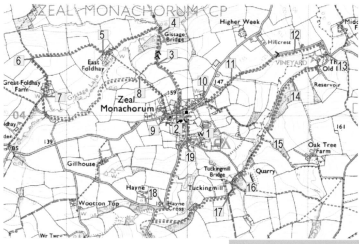

once hung (Wp.8 53M). Faced with two narrow paths heading off left and diagonally left, we create our own path, ascending to the top left field corner and through a gate beside a solitary tree.

Enjoying distant **Dartmoor** views at a lane, we go straight on down a paddock and over a stile into a sheltered path bending between houses into the village. Turning left (Wp.9 61M) to the **Zeal Monachorum** junction, we bear left in front of Sacristan Cottage and immediately right beside Monks Cottage continuing along a lane to the speed limit sign (Wp.10 66M). Going right down a 'Public Footpath' for 50 yards, then left over a stile, our path winds through rough pasture towards a barn; climbing a stile yellow arrows point us straight through the building and into a field. Heading down we cross into the next field, descending large boarded steps into a small valley to a combined stile and footbridge (Wp.11 71M). Climbing up the slope we stay beside the field hedge enjoying pleasant views along the **Yeo Valley** to the village of **Down St Mary** on the far hill.

Crossing a stile into Down St Mary vineyard we stay above the warm south facing terraced hillside, until 30 yards before the end of the hedge we go left over a stile (Wp.12 80M) and right down a lane to a bridge over the **River Yeo**. The vineyard shop next to The Old Mill sells several varieties of white wine including an award winner served during the Queen's Jubilee tour to Devon in 2002. Turning right (Wp.13 85M) onto a 'Public Footpath' we head along the valley floor past a barn and through a field into a wood (Wp.14 91M), sauntering along a cool pine scented path above the river to a path junction. Bearing left through a gate (Wp.15 97M) we follow yellow arrows through a field and copse onto a wide earth track that runs through a disused quarry to a road bridge at Tucking Mill (Wp.16 103M).

views open up to the village

Now 'Bridleway' signs point us straight on before we swing left for a few yards in front of a house, then fork right between hedges to the end of a little green track and through two gates. In front of us is a path fork (Wp.17 107M) and leaving the 'Bridleway', we go through a gate and bear right following yellow markers; staying beside a hedge we climb part way up the second field and go right through the second gate into a wood. Strolling gently down into pastures, views open up to the village as we bear away from the trees onto a lane; turning right we cross a bridge and past the village sign to **Hayne Cross** (Wp.18 120M). Going ahead for **Lapford** we climb the lane, slowing down as we reach the 30mph signs and turning first right (Wp.19 128M) to the **Waie Inn** (130M).

8 A Tiverton Triangle

The market town of **Tiverton** is our starting point for this splendid walk over rolling hills and along two totally contrasting valleys, the broad **Exe Valley** and its delightful **River Dart** tributary. Farming in this bucolic countryside is mainly dairy, beef and sheep; in summer the small fields change colour depending on whether the grass is being grazed or cut for hay and silage; this walk makes you realise just how many shades of green create such a marvellous patchwork quilt landscape.

Three shorter linear walks complete the triangle, with bus services to the start of each section. To miss out the initial long steady climb from **Tiverton** take the bus to **Withleigh** and walk down the quiet **Dart Valley** to **Bickleigh**. The return section from **Bickleigh** to **Tiverton** along the **Exe Valley** is the least demanding, although in wet weather the riverside and valley paths can get very muddy. **Tiverton** has cafes, pubs, a Castle, Museum and a modern glass interpretation of a Pannier Market.

Access by bus: No 55 between **Tiverton** to **Exeter** goes via **Bickleigh**.
No 346 from **Tiverton** to **Withleigh** (ask for the stop at the top of **Withleigh** just before the Parish Church sign)
Access by car: Parking is available in the town centre including a multi-storey car park beside the Bus Station; walk up Phoenix Lane and left along Fore Street**.**

Three Shorter Linear Walks
Tiverton-Withleigh from Wp.1 to Wp.5. 3.7 miles 5.9km A230M/D110m along quiet country lanes and tracks
Withleigh-Bickleigh from Wp.5 to Wp.19. 4.9 miles 7.9km A160m/D320m along a peaceful river valley on paths, fields, bridleway and lanes
Bickleigh-Tiverton from Wp.19. 3.9 miles 6.3km A95m/D55m along the **Exe Valley Way** on footpaths, tracks and a lane.

Facing the Italianate Town Hall (Wp.1 0M) (SS 954125) we keep right down Angel Hill over the **River Exe** and turn right at a mini roundabout into **West Exe**; the large building ahead is Heathcoat's textile factory, a major local employer. Turning left into Wellbrook Street then over a crossroads towards 'Seven Crosses' (Wp.2 6M) we reach Walrond's Almshouses built in 1597 by a wealthy cloth merchant. Strolling past the Fire Station we bear right, signed

'Broomhill' then turn left up Bakers Hill (Wp.3 12M), climbing resolutely up the original steep lane from **Tiverton** to **Withleigh**; with views back over the town we go straight on over a crossroads (Wp.4 34M) to a crest.

Enjoying distant vistas to **Exmoor** and the **Blackdown Hills** we descend to a junction, bear right for 200 yards to a Y-junction (Wp.5 43M) and fork left along a no through road. As the tarmac peters out we continue down a track into a valley and ignoring turnings, follow a rough track that winds up to a sharp road bend (Wp.6 58M). Crossing over onto an overgrown path, we climb up to a wider gravel track offering fine southern views to the ancient hill earthwork of **Cadbury Castle** and the **Raddon Hills**. At a lane in front of **Withleigh** village hall (Wp.7 70M) we turn left down to a T-junction at the B3137, carefully cross over and go left for 50 yards then swing sharp right into a no through lane (Wp.8 75M) (0M).

Descending to a small car park on our left we climb a stile onto National Trust grassland; this beautiful valley known locally as **Buzzards** is made up of deciduous woodland, steep pasture and water meadows. Heading half right downhill towards a shallow depression running down the opposite hillside we go through a gate (Wp.9 10M) midway along a hedge and bear left to the valley floor. Going between a wide gap along a raised field path we climb a stile into **Thongsleigh Wood** and after passing a footbridge, continue beside the **River Dart** until our path bends left along duckboards; the first 25 yard section ends at a low mound where we turn right along an old hedge bank (Wp.10 18M). Our path twists and turns onto the delightful river bank; you may find slots of red and roe deer in soft earth but the animals themselves are very shy. Joining an earth track our route bears right through a gate (Wp.11 25M) into a perfect picnic meadow; the track restarts half way along inside the left hedge, as we go ahead to a National Trust sign in **Cross's Wood**.

Ignoring a railed footbridge, we turn left for 40 yards, then right over an unsigned stile (Wp.12 31M) and plank bridge; going ahead along a field to a pedestrian gate tucked into the hedge we bear left, steadily climbing into **Huntland Wood** onto a broad contour path and a stunning array of springtime bluebells shimmering between mature trees. Dropping to a lane (Wp.13 45M) and turning right down to a road junction (Wp.14 48M) we go left towards 'Little Silver' and as the valley widens climb past Meadhayes to a crest. Forking left after 50 yards onto a 'Public Bridleway' (Wp.15

springtime bluebells

59M) our shaded path, always muddy after a wet spell, goes through a gate then descends between gnarled trees and gates to a grey roofed barn. Bearing right in front of a cottage and left on a lane for 30 yards, we fork right on a gravelled 'Public Bridleway' (Wp.16 69M) strolling past Upper Dart Cottage to the top of a wood and through a gate to be greeted with beautiful views towards **Bickleigh** and the **Exe Valley**.

The track is concreted for a short way as we descend past a cottage to the river and staying on the right bank follow a path through a double metal gate to a yellow marked gate on our left (Wp17 85M). Bearing right along a riverside meadow towards the far right corner our way is along a narrow path running behind bramble patches at the foot of the hillside; going through rough scrubland into a pasture, we continue on a raised bank beside a wood to a field gate (Wp18 94M). Bearing left on a lane to a T-junction, we turn left into the **Exe Valley** and the A396 **Exeter Tiverton** road at **Bickleigh Bridge** (Wp.19 102M) (0M)); above the cricket field on the left slope staked rows of vines produce grapes for the vinification of Yearlstone wines. Picturesque **Bickleigh** is a centuries old crossing point of the **River Exe** and a pleasant spot for a break offering a variety of eating places; the **Tiverton** bus stops on the left.

Crossing the five arched bridge beside the **Fisherman's Cott** we amble ahead to the second bridge beside **Bickleigh Mill** craft centre and turn left in front of Millhayes (Wp.20 4M). Our route to **Tiverton** is clearly marked by yellow public footpath signs and green V symbols of the **Exe Valley Way**; with the river on our left we enjoy an easy undulating path bowling along through woods and meadows before a final lane section into the town.

Going through a gate and tracking beside the leat into a wood we stay on the main path, climbing a little way before dropping back to the valley floor. Waymark signs point us left off the track over a stile into a large riverside

through trees to a stile

meadow; strolling beside the **Exe** watching canoeists glide downstream, we jink through a gateway and along the next field, then over a plank and stile into a wood. Following a pleasant riverside path to a stile we bear left up a field slope through trees to a stile; our undulating path again returns to the riverside before gradually swinging between a field and woodland and ascending through two gates (Wp.21 43M) on either side of a small valley.

Our broad track continues ahead to an **Exe Valley Way** marker pointing us left to a stile on the tree edge. Going straight on along a sloping field and staying to the right of a line of trees we turn left through a gate; turning right, beside the Water Treatment Works, our route is over a stile onto a short fenced path to a concrete lane (Wp.22 56M). From here a level lane takes us past Lower Collipriest Farm to a Y-junction on the outskirts of **Tiverton** where we fork left (Wp.23 66M) into St Andrews Street; the early 19th century cottages were built for Heathcoat factory workers. Climbing beside the Bridewell, once the towns combined police station and prison, we cross a footbridge, passing the Museum, a school in a former life with separate boys and girls entrances, and return to the Town Hall (81M).

Tiverton Town Hall

Fancy some typically beautiful English countryside, great views and some real exercise? Then this walk on the **Blackdown** escarpment is the one for you. Starting from the pretty village of **Culmstock** we make two good climbs to **Culmstock Beacon** and **Wellington Hill** - both with their own historical interest quite apart from their fantastic views. And then to return, we stroll through gorgeous meadows and woods finally accompanying the lazy **River Culm** back to our start.

Access by car: Exit M5 at junction 27 and take A38 east towards **Wellington**. After 4 miles and just after crossing the M5, turn right on the B3391 opposite the **Woodlands Business Park** and follow the road for 2 miles to **Culmstock** parking by the church.

From the church (Wp.1 0M) we stroll down to the **Great War Memorial** and turn right on the **Strand** following the **River Culm** which we cross via its pretty arched bridge. Ignoring the **Culm Valley Inn** for now we leave the B3391 **Tiverton** road as it curves left and continue straight keeping **Culmstock School** on our left (Wp.2 6M)) steadily uphill out of **Millmoor**. After 400yds we take a small lane right (Wp.3 12M) passing **Knap House** and soon catch our first view of **Culmstock Beacon**

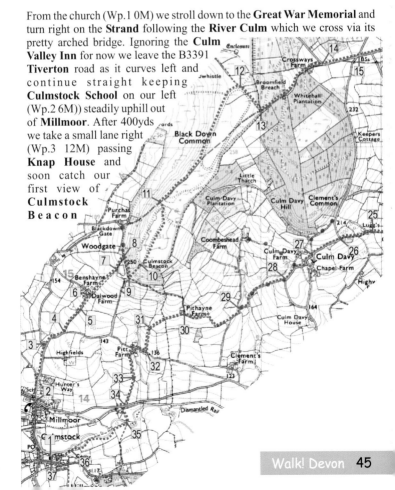

with what looks like a beehive on its top. At a wooden signpost we take a yellow waymarked public footpath left (Wp.4 14M), the grassy farm track leading towards **Dalwood Farm,** but just before the farm we negotiate a small stile (Wp.5 18M) and cut across the field on the right thus avoiding a visit to the farmhouse. However, we are not deprived of the delights of the farmyard! Exiting the field over another stile (Wp.6 20M) we strike out through the muddy yard, maintaining direction (NE) and keeping broadly to the left-hand side of the field, still uphill. A yellow waymarked metal gate (Wp.7 26M) leads us into a little wilderness from where we emerge over a stile into a small wooded area and a T-junction (Wp.8 29M) at which we turn right on a public footpath. As the fenced-off enclosure on the right comes to an end, we find a narrow path on the left towards a gate (Wp.9 32M) and follow the rough track up and to the left through trees out onto the open hillside. We puff our way up on a steep flinty path through bracken to arrive at that beehive - **Culmstock Beacon** (Wp.10 38M) to admire the fabulous view and peruse the interesting information boards at the trig point.

Culmstock Beacon

The stone beehive shaped hut, thought to be the only one to survive, was built in 1588 to enclose the Pole Beacon erected on the hill. The hut kept beacon keepers dry while watching for fires on adjacent beacon hills - chains of beacons famously once spreading the alarm at the approach of the Spanish Armada.

There seem to be any number of paths leaving the beacon so, from the clearing and with the beehive on our left we take the left fork ahead (NNE) heading to the right of the distant mast and keeping close to the gorse bushes. Now we can step out - the walking is level and easy on a broad grassy way and we have glorious views of Devon countryside, our path swinging to the left after 500yds as we're joined by a track from the right. Through silver birch we arrive at a track junction by a pond (perhaps a good picnic spot) (Wp.11 48M) to turn right on the main path heading straight towards the mast (NE). We're up and away from it all as we stride along **Black Down Common** escarpment accompanied by stonechats and the occasional

pony and, as the path loops to the right at the next pond (Wp.12 61M), we continue with it (SE) for another 100yds towards the mast and trees. A small muddy path then takes us left off the broad track through low gorse to trees (Wp.13 63M) where our route takes us left and through a small metal gate onto a public bridleway lined with beech. With private woodland to the left and the conifers of **Whitehall Plantation** to our right we pass the access track to the mast on the right (a modern contrast to the simpler communication method used at **Culmstock Beacon**!) and bear left down to **Crossways Farm** and the lane ahead (Wp.14 73M). Continuing straight along the lane we now trespass into Somerset and after ignoring a right turn to **Culmstock** we approach a major junction (Wp.15 77M); here we maintain our direction towards **Hemyock**. The road is quite fast but visibility is good and we proceed with care for 500yds to a wooden signpost (Wp.16 83M) taking us left along a stony public bridleway towards trees. A two minute stroll brings us to a choice of gates - we select the one to the right into National Trust land towards the **Wellington Monument** for a delightful meander in shady mixed bluebell woods, contouring around the hill.

Wellington Monument

The monument was completed in 1892 in honour of Arthur Wellesley, the Duke of Wellington, to commemorate his famous victory at the Battle of Waterloo. The triangular structure was originally intended to be topped with a statue of the Duke but, after a chequered history of development, plans were finally redrawn resulting in the 175 foot structure adorning the hill top today. A spiral 235 step staircase, not for the faint hearted, leads to an observation point at the top and the views from there are said to be stupendous! Currently the lower parts of the tower are shrouded in corrugated panels due to structural defects to the staircase but hopefully it will be reopened soon.

Coming to a pair of metal gates in the midst of beech and chestnut trees (Wp.17 95M) we turn right on a steep path which happily quickly turns to steps and there it is, towering in front of us, **Wellington Monument** (Wp.18 99M). We set off picking up the main track in front of the tower to the left (SE) onto the broad leafy avenue of **Firs Plantation** to arrive at a green barrier, a car park and the road (Wp.19 107M). Turning right into a beechy tunnel we bend a little left with the road and then as it starts to drop and curve right we spot our public footpath sign to the left and follow it over a stile into a field (Wp.20 114M). A second stile takes us into a grassy corridor and we now begin a delightful section of the walk as we wander south past gorgeous bluebell woods dropping away to the right with stunning distant views beyond. Four stiles later we come across an isolated summerhouse with a truly exquisite outlook, a good place to reflect before continuing on our easy level rambling through a couple more gate/stiles down to a road (Wp.21 135M).

A right turn leads us down a leafy lane for 200yds where we go right at the next junction (Wp.22 139M) between neat hedges to **Culm Pyne Barton** with its interesting warning sign.

Directly opposite the house gate on the right of the lane is a small signpost nestling by an oak tree, (Wp.23 143M) together with a rusted gate leading into an orchard and we head for the apples! A couple of fields later and, in our case, after a good chasing by some bullocks, we exit through a gate onto a farm track taking us up and left round to **Goodall's Farm** (Wp.24 155M). Keeping the silo and barn to our left, we head up towards the chicken run and following it to the right join the free range chickens through a wire mesh gate for a stroll up the hill together. We escape the fowl through a second mesh gate (Wp.25 157M) onto an earthy track leading us to the pretty hamlet of **Luggs,** a cattle grid eventually taking us out onto a lane where we turn left (Wp.26 161M). Our next choice is at **Culm Davy** (Wp.27 164M) and we take the tiny lane just to the right of **Chapel Cottage** (SW), keeping on past the thatched cottage with the fox on top. Round to the left with the lane then we fork right onto a broken-up track (Wp.28 168M) going downhill through gorgeous wild flowers and over a stream to a T-junction (Wp.29 174M). Turning left for 100yds we branch off right on a public footpath and then left again as the footpath forks at **Pithayne Farm** (Wp.30 181M). Leaving with the farmhouse behind us through a gate following yellow waymarks into pasture (E), we take an indistinct path under telegraph wires to a pair of wooden gates opposite and then bear gently left to the corner of the field by a big ash tree (Wp.31 187M). Through the gate we keep to the right-hand hedge-line to the bottom of the field and go right at yet another gate towards **Pitt Farm**. Just past the stone farm buildings we turn left on a yellow waymarked public footpath (Wp.32 191M), through a white ornamental gate and across the tussocky field (S) towards a small dip in the hedge and a rusty gate. A small stile lurks in the hedge to our right (Wp.33 196M) and, negotiating it, we set off diagonally heading for a modern cream-coloured house and the road below (Wp.34 200M). We're going round three sides of the house, **Blackwater** (right on the road then left, left) and emerge over a stile to

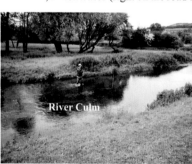

a wooden footbridge over the **River Culm** (Wp.35 203M). Some gorgeous picnic/rest spots here - but we tear ourselves away past the fly fishermen to meander with the river to a metal footbridge (Wp.36 211M).

We stick to the left through a kissing gate or two and following the path find ourselves safely back to **Culmstock** churh and our starting point (Wp.37 214M).

The flat topped **Blackdown Hills** stretching along the Devon, Somerset border are designated an Area of Outstanding Natural Beauty and provide fine year round walking; the westerly facing wooded escarpment drops steeply into the broad agricultural **Culm Valley**.

Our walk takes us along the hillside to **Blackborough** then on field paths, tracks and quiet lanes through the cob and thatched villages of **Kentisbeare** and **Broadhembury**. If the weather is fine during our final steady climb to the ridge, the gliders of the Devon and Somerset Gliding Club are likely to a feature. If you walk this route from mid summer we will be amazed if you finish without purple stained fingers, the high hedgerows offer a real blackberry fest - a stick is useful as the juiciest ones are always just out of reach!

Access by car: from Junction 25 of M5 near **Cullompton** take A373 towards **Honiton**. After 3 miles, pass **Keepers Cottage** pub and take first left towards **Sheldon** for 2 miles. As lane bends left steeply uphill, look for Woodland Trust car park with height restrictor on left side (ST 095069).

Shorter walk A: Follow walk to Priory Wall Cross roads shortly after Wp.13 and turn left up the lane for 1.4 miles to the car park 8 miles/12.8km A250m/D250m

Shorter walk B: From car park turn right down the lane for 1.4 miles to the third turning on the left at Priory Wall Cross roads and turn left towards **Kerswell** 6.1 miles/9.8km A235m/D235m

Strolls: along the escarpment as far as you like and back to the car park.

Starting from the car park we go through a gate (Wp.1 0M) into Rhododendron Wood strolling along a level 'Bridleway' with winter views across the **Culm Valley**; our well used route runs along the side of the **Blackdown Hills** escarpment to a bridleway intersection (Wp.2 18M) and continues straight on to a metalled lane (Wp.3 25M). Going ahead onto a 'Public Footpath' and climbing a few paces to a fork, we follow the left yellow arrow, snaking between deciduous trees then crossing stiles either side of a belt of conifers before dropping between large beeches to a path T-junction. Turning left down a banked path to a road (Wp.4 35M) and straight across past **Blackborough's** information board, we go right along a no through road to a pair of 'Public Footpath' signs at a gate on our left (Wp.5 38M).

Following the direction of the right hand sign to the edge

of the escarpment we head down the middle of the field and through a gap in a hedgebank aiming for an earth scar at the bottom of the hill. Big views stretch across the **Culm Valley** to the distant **Dartmoor** skyline while to our left the steep wooded **Blackdown Hills** curve south to **Broadhembury**. Climbing left over a stile (Wp.6 44M) we go along a narrow sunken *green lane* to a track junction and ignoring the green 'Footpath' sign, <u>keep right, as indicated by the yellow arrow</u> (Wp.7 46M). After negotiating a muddy section, we head past a farmhouse and on to Mortimers Cross; strolling ahead our easy lane walking continues past a monkey puzzle tree to a walled road junction, where we bend left to a track on our right (Wp.8 68M).

climbing between high hedges

Turning right and climbing between overgrown high hedges, we go straight across a lane and along a clearer gravel surface, pausing to look back to the escarpment and gliders making lazy circles in the sky. Striding out between banks our track bends left and right before entering open countryside and joining a road. Going straight on past a pretty house named Wressing, we fork left at a Y-junction (Wp.9 83M) for 100 yards, then turn left along a lane crossing a footbridge or splashing through a ford to Goodiford Cross. Turning left past Goodiford Mill and left at a 'Public Footpath' sign (Wp.10 93M) we head through a fishermen's car park to a green barn, going left and immediately right over a brook along a grass path beside the last of the lakes. Ignoring a stile in the hedge we bear right beside wooden railings and climb a stile into **Silver Wood**, created by the Woodland Trust in 1999 as a Millennium community project. Crossing duckboards and a bridge, we go left on a grass path to a lane (Wp.11 107M) bearing right then left up Silver Street into **Kentisbeare**. The Priesthall, a fine medieval Church-

House, stands near the 15th century parish church of **St Mary** which has a wide rood screen and a checkered stone tower.

Our way continues straight on through the square to a Y-junction, keeping left for **Blackborough** past Honest Heart Cross to a sharp left bend (Wp.12 116M); going ahead along a track to a 'Public Footpath' sign we bear right through a gate, staying beside the right hedge to a stile. Maintaining the same direction across a field to the far left corner, we swing gradually left up a smaller field to a gate beside a white road sign (Wp.13 126M). Turning right, climbing to Priory Wall Cross (the short walk turns left) we keep straight on for **Kerswell** down a high banked shaded lane. To our right beyond the lakes, Carswell Priory was for many centuries the site of a monastic cell of the Cluniac order. At Matthews Cross we go left into the hamlet of **Kerswell** following a winding road past the red telephone box to the second road junction, turning left for a few paces to a gravelled area and a 'Public Footpath' sign on our right (Wp.14 148M).

Sauntering right along a track to a house, we pick up yellow arrows pointing us over a couple of railway sleepers onto an overgrown path that meanders through delightful woodland to a field edge. Following footpath signs we go across a pasture, keep left through a short field and halfway along the left hedge of a third, cross a stile and climb diagonally right to a lane. The flat landscape and red fertile soil of the **Culm Valley** supports arable crops as well dairy farming.

cross a stile

Turning right along a lane for 7 minutes to a footpath sign on our left (Wp.15 169M) we climb a flight of stone steps, keeping beside the left fence towards **Broadhembury Church**; where the boundary fence goes sharp left, we bear gradually right across the field to a hedge corner and stile. Staying beside a hedge, a path brings us to a lane where we turn left between pretty cottages to a road junction in **Broadhembury** (Wp.16 181M); to visit the 13th century **St Andrews Church** and **Drewe Arms** keep right between thatched cottages and return to this point. Forking left up a lane we start our ascent, climbing to a stile (Wp.17 187M) opposite Hembercombe Farm and turning left into a large pasture.

spectacular panorama to Hembury Hill

Trudging straight up the slope towards lofty hills, we arrive at a stile in the top left corner then go across a field and along a short track; time to admire a spectacular panorama to **Hembury Hill** *Iron Age* fort and East Devon's flat topped ridges. Now following waymarks we bear right into a field beside a hedge, go through a copse, then head across another

field and over a stile. Turning right up a pine scented path and cutting across the contours at an angle it's easier going as we pass enormous beeches before emerging through a gate (Wp.18 213M) onto an active airfield. Turning left onto cropped turf and heeding warnings to keep close to the boundary we stroll to a stile in the left corner accompanied by the whirring winch cable launching gliders skywards. Going through a gate our path initially drops into trees before climbing back up through gorse and bracken to a road (Wp.19 231M) where we turn left down to the car park (234M).

The Whetstoners of Blackborough

Whetstone mining flourished along the escarpment for 200 years until about 1910; the Whetstoners dug horizontal adits by hand into the hillside, sometimes as far as 400 yards to extract harder lumps of stone from the soft greensand. From these concretions, high quality abrasive stones known as Devonshire Batts were manufactured and used for sharpening blades in England and abroad. The remains of the collapsed mines are on the right of the escarpment path and at **Blackborough** there are more details on the information board.

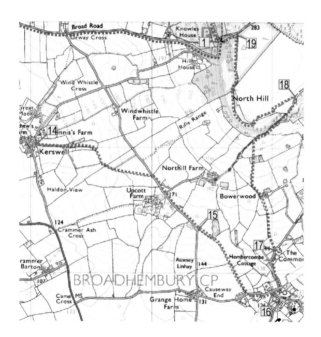

The countryside around **Stockland** is just typical of gentle Devon. On this walk we ramble through lush farmland and alongside tinkling streams and rivers, a couple of good climbs rewarding our struggles with glorious views. **Stockland Great Castle Fort** (or Camp as some name it) can be picked out across the way on its hillside and we visit the remains of **Stockland Little Castle** as we meander back to the pretty village of **Stockland**. Here the lovely 15th century church of **St Michael and All Angels** awaits us and from there the **Kings Arms Inn** is always a temptation on our way back to the start.

Access by car: From the A30, 5 miles NW of **Honiton** (and just before the A303 splits off), take the right turning towards **Stockland**. After 2 miles take the second left to **Stockland** and continue through the village towards **Membury**. After 500 yards park on the right at **Cokers Elm Cross**.

Leaving **Cokers Elm Cross** (Wp.1 0M) to the left (NE) we head out along a public footpath between high hedges and, over a stile, keep left in the field alongside the hedge. A gentle downhill stroll crunching the acorns underfoot, brings us to a wooden footbridge across the **River Yarty** (Wp.2 9M) and then another rickety footbridge in the hedge takes us across the meadow to a small five bar gate. Following the yellow waymarks directly ahead we negotiate yet another footbridge (and there are more to come!) quickly coming to a stile/footbridge on the right (Wp.3 15M) where we turn right over the stile and continue straight with the hedge on our left. A level stretch of lush grass soothes us as waymarks lead us to the left into the adjacent field which we traverse diagonally towards the white buildings over on the right, **North Mill Dairy Farm**. We aim slightly uphill for the signpost taking us around the left back of the barn, over a stile and along a fenced path and driveway where we emerge at a lane (Wp.4 24M).

Turning right and just 50 yards past thatched cottages we take the public footpath to the right (Wp.5 26M) through a gate, with a small wooden shed on the right and hedge on the left. Yellow waymarks direct us towards a stream (luscious fungi are to be found around here in the autumn) and after one more footbridge we arrive at a road to rejoin the **Yarty** at **Case Bridge** (Wp.6 30M). Straight across we follow the footpath running alongside the river, the ground well puddied up at our next footbridge, for a lovely meander maintaining our direction always towards **Waterhouse Farm** by wooden horse jumps to a gate in trees ahead. Skirting round to the left of the cream farmhouse, three stiles and a gate bring us to the lane (Wp.7 44M) where we turn right towards the house and then, as the lane bends right at **Old Orchard** bungalow, we continue straight between high hedges on a grassy track. Through a gate we come into a field and after a gentle uphill we're on a sunken track, trees either side and a patchwork of fields rising on the right. A concrete driveway (Wp.8 50M) leads us right towards **Yarty Farm** and we follow through the old farm buildings until at the end of the track (Wp.9 53M) we bear off left on a stony grassy driveway into trees, keeping the houses on our right. Ignoring a fork to the left we continue through a metal gate diagonally across the meadow to another gate and, with the river on our right, we enjoy a gorgeous stroll across the fields finally exiting through a metal gate onto the lane at **Beckford Bridge** (Wp.10 67M).

A right turn brings us to **Beckford Cross** where we continue straight over the road onto a stony track and after 20 yards fork right off the track through a gate and into a field. The tempting valley on the right is hard to resist but resolutely we keep to the left up the steeper part of the hill, heading for the small gate to the left of the trees at the top of the field. At the gate (Wp.11 74M) we turn right still steadily uphill towards the power lines on the brow of the hill and then cut across left towards an exit gate by an enormous pylon. Bearing right under the power lines on **Dalwood Lane** we climb past **Thorny Cleave** with **Danes Hill** to our left and as the track levels out we come to the road at **Danes Hill Cross** (Wp.12 87M). Here we turn right towards **Heathstock** on the metalled road, past **Daneshill House** and back under the power lines, climbing gradually until we come to **Little Acres** (Wp.13 93M) with a public footpath to the sharp left and a bridleway to the left. We take the bridleway left towards Hawks Hill, the broad stony access track wandering up and down then, in trees and just past **Hawks Hill** bungalow, we take the turning to the right (Wp.14 97M). A brisk climb up the steep muddy path and

Beckford Bridge

five minutes later we are at the top with the trees dropping away on the left and great views beyond - the ridge of **Horner Hill** is a superb place for a picnic (there is a wooden bench if you go on a bit). Coming into gorse we start our descent into pleasant shady trees and, as the track forks (Wp.15 106M), we go right on a stony pathway eventually leaving the trees at a gate and onto a blue waymarked public bridleway. Ambling along the easy, broad, grassy path in and out of woodland, a gate with a blue bridleway sign (Wp.16 116M) leads us round to the left on a broad muddy track and, with the trees to our left, down to the lane at **Sandpitts** (Wp.17 120M). Here we can catch a good sighting of **Stockland Great Castle Fort** to the left - it's the dark clump of trees sticking out in the large field directly opposite and to the west. It's quite a relief after our exertions to stroll left gently down the quiet little lane enjoying the lovely views before coming to the road junction at **Heathstock** (Wp.18 129M) where the delightful sign on the porch of the cream and pink house points us right towards **Stockland**.

After one minute we turn left at a cream thatched cottage down a muddy track

through farm buildings, bending right with the stony track downhill as we leave the last building. We emerge to a lane (Wp.19 136M) and turn right then left after 200yards at **Ford Cross** down the lane past **Ford Farm**, continuing over the stream and uphill ignoring the drive on the left as we level out. At the T-junction (Wp.20 147M) we take the right towards **Millhayes** and then after 50yards turn left on a track with high hedges gently uphill, passing by a stile on the left and following round to the right. As we come into a few trees our path forks and we diverge left up a broad grassy track, greeted and escorted by friendly dogs to **Mount Pleasant Farm** and a lane (Wp.21 162M). We maintain our direction uphill on the tarmac road and, almost at the top of the rise and as the trees on the right finish, we turn right on a footpath through a metal gate (Wp.22 168M) down the side of the wood. Just after the trees on our right end and in the field to our left we can see the ramparts of **Stockland Little Castle**, a circular raised grassy bank - a lovely spot and well worth investigating (Wp.23 171M). Continuing down the field with the Castle on our left, we take the rightmost of a pair of metal gates downhill between hedges, and then fork left diagonally across a field to a lane (Wp.24 179M). We turn left and follow the road to the right and down, ignoring turnings to the left and right, past

pretty thatched **Mayes Cottage**, over the stream and then uphill past farm buildings to a T-junction (Wp.25 186M). The view of **Stockland Church** gives us just the impetus we need to turn right and after 50 yards left through a metal gate on a footpath into a grassy field. Yellow waymarks lead us gently downhill towards the church across the meadows and we arrive at the churchyard (Wp.26 202M) to admire the handsome turnstile.

Stockland Church

Stockland Village Cross is our final decision point (Wp.27 205M) and, after a possible refreshment stop at the **Kings Arms Inn**, we turn right towards **Membury** passing the school and back to our parking place (Wp.28 211M).

This excursion begins with a nostalgic ride on the historic **Seaton** tramway followed by a bracing walk along the coastal path to the pretty village of **Beer**. Heading inland we experience peaceful Devon countryside, a possible visit to the **Beer Quarry** caves, and then a stroll along the wooded **Morganhayes C o v e r t** ridge before meandering back to **Colyford**.

3 | 3¼H | 9 miles/14km | 230m / 210m | 3

Access by car: Park in **Colyton** at the **Tramway** carpark

We start this expedition with a 25 minute ride on the famous miniature tramway down the **Axe** estuary to **Seaton.**

The **Seaton Tramway**, opened in 1970, runs 3miles from **Colyton** to **Seaton** following the **River Axe** and provides excellent bird watching over the estuary salt marshes. The narrow gauge trams are about half the size of those common in the first half of the last century in many towns and originally ran along the seafront at **Eastbourne**. They were moved to the **Seaton** site after the **Southern Railway** connection to the town closed in 1966 as part of the infamous Beeching cuts. The trams offer a full service between April and October with occasional trips during the rest of the year, currently costing £5.25 for the one way trip

Leaving the tram station in **Seaton** town centre (Wp.1 0M) we bear left at a roundabout heading south along **Harbour Road** turning right onto a busy street parallel to the seafront. At a T-junction we turn left to the sea then right on **Seaton West Walk,** a promenade at the back of the pebbly beach taking us to the **Chine Café** (Wp.2 9M) (note at low tide it is possible to continue on the beach turning right at **Seaton Hole** at the far end). We turn right following coastal path signs up a cleft in the cliff going left on the cliff top road then bearing left down **Old Beer Road** (Wp.3 15M). The road passes between houses then drops towards **Seaton Hole**, a café on the left and path coming up from the beach (Wp.4 20M). We turn left off the road past **Lew Hollow** climbing steeply up **Beer Hill** on a small wooded lane. After 200yds (Wp.5 23M) we turn sharply back on ourselves left on a footpath that makes its way across to the cliff edge then swings right following the hedge. The occasional break in the

Beer

bushes provides panoramic views of **Seaton** sheltering in the bay below.

After a brief level section we begin our descent steeply towards **Beer**, joining the beach road by the **Anchor Inn** (Wp.6 35M) and turning right away from the sea up **Fore Street**. The picturesque and bustling old fishing village offers plenty of opportunities for refreshment and browsing or even a diversion to the beach for a laze and gaze.

At the junction by the church we follow the road round to the left on **Causeway** signed 'All Routes' (Wp.7 39M) then after 200yds we bear left again to **Branscombe** passing a pair of golden lions guarding the house on the left and a terrace of finely decorated **Alms Houses** built in 1821 by Lord Rolle on the right. The famous **Beer Quarry Caves** (well worth a visit if time permits) are to be found 1mile along this lane; however, before reaching them we take a right towards **Beer Youth Hostel** (Wp.8 46M) then fork left along a broad stony track, one of Devon's famous *green lanes*.

Beer underground quarries covering an area of about 50 football pitches were worked continuously from Roman times until the beginning of the 20C - although even today the occasional block is extracted for restoration work. **Beer** stone is particularly suited for carving being relatively soft when first cut but hardening up on exposure to air, explaining why it has been used so extensively for historic and prestigious buildings up and down the country including **Exeter Cathedral**, **St Paul's Cathedral**, **Westminster Abbey,** the **Tower of London** and **Windsor Castle**.

We crunch uphill on weird shaped flint nodules, passing **Bovey Lane** water bore hole on the right, used to extract drinking water from the underlying aquifer. From high banks and tranquil woodland we come to a road (Wp.9 66M) with the grand **Bovey House** directly in front and we turn right. Still climbing we cross the busy B3174 **Hollyhead Road** (Wp.10 70M) coming to the A3052 (Wp.11 78M) at **Stafford Cross** where we again go carefully straight across towards **Colyton**.

Within 150yds we take a gate on the left onto a public footpath (Wp.12 81M) and strike out (NW) directly over a pony paddock making for a wooden gate in the hedge opposite taking us onto the **Axbridge** Point to Point course. Keeping to the low hedge on the left we make for a stile and small gate into the woods ahead (Wp.13 87M). The footpath sign indicates that we continue (NW) on a path between the conifers gently downhill, intersecting a large forestry track after 150yds (Wp.14 89M) where we turn right through a broken 5-bar gate. Still in conifers we stroll on the flinty track enjoying the birdsong and possibly sighting deer amidst a prolific sea of bluebells. We carry straight on at a cross tracks (Wp.15 93M) picking our way around deep ruts and frogspawn laden puddles, now in mixed woodland bedecked with lovely wild flowers. As our track splits (Wp.16 105M) we go right steadily uphill and on reaching the top of the incline we come to a large turning area for forestry machines (Wp.17 111M). To continue along the ridge would mean passing through the private **Jobbles Wood** so we divert, swinging back on ourselves (SSW) on a level track back through conifers onto the lane (Wp.18 118M) opposite **Leacroft Farm Caravan and Camping** site.

Turning left we stride out on the lane taking in the extensive views (SE) across **Seaton Bay** and the **Axe** valley. After ¾ mile we come to **White Gate** cross roads (Wp.19 129M) and turn left, signed' Whitwell Farm', on a broad gravel track lined with banks of bluebells and with glorious views heading north.

Reaching the trees and cross tracks we see a path exiting from **Jobbles Wood** on the left (Wp.20 136M) and we fork right following a signed public footpath along the edge of a conifer wood on the left and with open fields right. Two stiles, one to the right then one left take us into fields (Wp.21 141M) and we follow the hedge line downhill to yet another stile onto a narrow earthy track (Wp.22 144M). Continuing downhill the path snakes its way through wild natural woodland, occasionally quite boggy, where we're confronted by the many paths tried by those before us who aimed to keep dry feet!

All ways eventually lead to a kissing gate (Wp.23 154M) onto a lane which we cross (N), then after a few yards cross a second lane on to a bridleway signed 'Heathhayne Farm'. The track leads down to the stunning thatched farmhouse where we are greeted by numerous friendly hens overseen by a handsome cock and continues downhill between hedges through a gate to the **River Coly** (Wp.24 159M). We turn left following the river bank for 100yds to a wooden footbridge which we cross and then turn right back along the bank heading for **Colyton Church** through the riverside meadows. We exit the fields through a

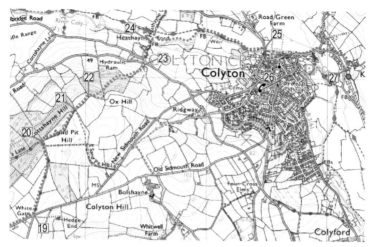

Colyton Bridge

small gate (Wp.25 176M) turning right over a road bridge, then left after 20yds by **Chantry Cottage**.

Opposite the imposing **Colyton House** entrance gates (Wp.26 179M) we turn left into **Rosemary Lane**, keeping the octagonal church tower on our right and passing the **Gerrard Arms**. We pick up signs for the tramway station which take us left along **Dolphin Street**, over a second river bridge and then right into **Station Road** back to the tramway carpark (Wp.27 191M)

This stretch of coast offers wonderful energetic cliff walking, some steep climbs and magnificent panoramas. East Devon's designation as an Area of Outstanding Natural Beauty has been strengthened since the **Jurassic Coast** was awarded status as a UNESCO World Heritage Site because of its unique geological timeline. See Box in Walk 15.

Our route starts from **Seaton Hole**, heading through the fishing village of **Beer** then along high cliffs to fabulous views at **Beer Head**; a steep descent enables us to explore an amazing tropical jungle covering the **Under Hooken Landslip**, before we continue to unspoilt **Branscombe Mouth.** Climbing the coastal heights to **Berry Camp Fort** we have a valley stroll to **Branscombe** with its fine church and working forge before a stiff climb onto **Hooken Cliffs** and a return via **Beer** to **Seaton Hole**.

* descending Under Hooken after Wp.6

Shorter walk A: Start and finish at Wp.5 in the car park above **Beer.**

8 miles/12.9km, A & D 380m.
Shorter walk B: Start at Wp.5 in the car park above **Beer**; walk to **Branscombe Mouth** Wp.8 and return from Wp.16. 4 miles/6.4km, A & D 225m.

Access by bus to Beer: No X53 Jurassic Coastlink between **Exeter** and **Poole**. No 899 between **Sidmouth** and **Seaton**. Walk through village to the **Anchor Inn** at Wp.4
Access by car: **Seaton Hole** is 28 miles from **Exeter**. Take A3052 towards **Lyme Regis** turning right on B3174 to **Beer** then on B3172 towards **Seaton** for 1 mile and turn right for **Seaton Hole**. Park on roadside above café.

Beer

From a signpost beside the Cliffside Refreshment Cabin (Wp.1 0M) (SY235897), guided by Acorn tipped signs, we follow the 'Beer coastpath', climbing part way up Beer Hill lane before turning left onto a tarmac path (Wp.2 4M). Swinging up to a cliff top, early morning mists disappear, giving us our first views over **Lyme Bay**, and starting downhill we can see stark white cliffs encircling the fishing boats pulled up on **Beer's** pebble beach. Beneath trees we continue straight on at a sign post (Wp.3 13M) along the 'Coast Path', descending a series of winding concrete steps to a children's play park. Keeping left in front of the **Anchor Inn** for 'Branscombe', the 'Coast path link' (Wp.4 17M) climbs Common Lane alongside a row of flint and pebble cottages to a car park - the start and finish for shorter walks A and B.

Bearing left into Little Lane (Wp.5 22M) for 'Branscombe Mouth' we head towards tiered rows of caravans and curve left down a path and out into fields. Our well trodden route gradually climbs beside hedges through kissing gates and pastures to **Beer Head** where we aim for a kissing gate in the top right field corner beside the cliff edge. This excellent vantage point gives wonderful views of the **Under Hooken Landslip** and a superb panorama of **Lyme Bay**. Drawing level with three coastal pinnacles off to our left, we dip to a kissing gate (Wp.6 41M) and go left down a narrow 'Branscombe Mouth coastpath'; at the first bend is a splendidly positioned bench - thank you Kate and Derek.

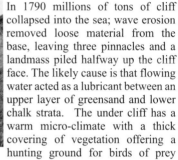

Under Hooken Landslip

In 1790 millions of tons of cliff collapsed into the sea; wave erosion removed loose material from the base, leaving three pinnacles and a landmass piled halfway up the cliff face. The likely cause is that flowing water acted as a lubricant between an upper layer of greensand and lower chalk strata. The under cliff has a warm micro-climate with a thick covering of vegetation offering a hunting ground for birds of prey while the sea cliffs provide nests for fulmars. If you enjoy this type of hemmed in walking with constant twists and turns there is a 7 mile undercliff between **Lyme Regis** and **Seaton**, but for us the **Under Hooken Landslip** is long enough.

After a winding stepped descent halfway down the cliffs, we are enveloped by green luxuriant vegetation beneath a jungle canopy; in these warm climes, ivy clings to trees like rampant tropical lianas and although the sea isn't visible, the sound of crashing waves reverberates off rock faces. Dropping to sea level we can either crunch along the pebbles or in our case continue on an undulating earth path, gradually climbing through a caravan park to a cattle grid (Wp.7 63M) before turning left down to **Branscombe Mouth**. Crossing a stream in front of the Sea Shanty seasonal cafe we bear right onto National Trust land at **West Cliff** (Wp.8 68M) and taking the 'Western Mouth Coast path' keep right of a stone retaining wall before swinging left up a steep slope to a gate. Bearing left up steps (Wp.9 73M) near the cliff edge it's a puff and grunt ascent to the field edges where we change gear, striding along a broad

woodland path with inland glimpses to a junction for 'Western Mouth' (Wp.10 91M). Turning left along the 'Coastpath' past a ramshackle outbuilding we bear right, climbing to open cliff tops, then on a level grass path beside field edges pass the low gorse covered banks of **Berry Camp Fort** enjoying coastal views to **Sidmouth**. At a kissing gate we go into a long field and just beyond two large clumps of gorse arrive at a small marker post (Wp.11 104M) displaying two yellow arrows pointing ahead and left. Ignoring both and leaving the coastpath, our unsigned route turns acutely right, as we head back across the pasture along a faint grass track,

views to Sidmouth

crossing a broken down boundary and curving left to a gate in the field corner. Picking up a 'Public footpath' sign we head along a track to Berry Barton caravan site, going right between farm buildings to a lane (Wp.12 114M) and turning right down to **Street** (Wp.13 120M); the **Fountain Head** pub serves good food and as a bonus has its own micro brewery.

After going right between cottages at a T-junction and strolling gently downhill past a Millennium Rose Garden, views open to the Church and the pretty linear village of **Branscombe**. **St Winifred's Church**, believed to be of Saxon origin, has a lovely valley setting and the light interior is exceptionally well kept; plaster has been cut away in places, exposing sections of English and Norman stonework. Continuing ahead to a working forge (Wp.14 135M) we turn off right on a grass path beside the Bakery and after crossing a footbridge, bear left along a *leat* to Manor Mill and it's *overshot water wheel*. Going left to a path intersection (Wp.15 140M) and turning right for 'Branscombe Mouth' we stroll on a level gravel path to a Y-junction (keep left for the village

Branscombe

and **Masons Arms**); forking right along a footpath to the beach, we turn left in front of the café.

views back along the coast

Somewhat daunted by the thought of climbing **East Cliff**, we cross the stream and bear right for 'Beer' (Wp.16 153M), trudging up an unremitting steep incline until a long flight of steps delivers us to onto **Hooken Cliffs**. Rewarded by fine views back along the coast and up the **Branscombe** valley a 'Public Bridleway' marker directs us ahead through double gates into a long pasture; from here, thankfully, it's a level hike to the old coast guard lookout (Wp.18 176M) and a 'Bridleway' sign. Going half left, but not as far left as the signpost indicates, we follow a narrow path which widens to a farm track, gradually bearing left over cattle grids to a lane; there are fine views over **Seaton**, the **Axe Estuary** and along terracotta coloured under cliffs to **Lyme Regis**. Descending a tarmac lane past the car park, we continue down Common Lane into **Beer** then turn left beside the toilets (Wp.18 195M) up the self explanatory 'Public Footpath to Seaton avoiding steep steps'. Climbing to a path junction at the tree edge we turn right for 'Seaton' to rejoin our outward route at Wp.3 and after cresting a final cliff top, descend to Beer Hill lane and turn right to **Seaton Hole** (211M).

East Devon countryside at its best. This varied walk starts at the delightful village of **Ottery St Mary** and heads off to the imposing **East Hill** ridge for a stretch through woods with far reaching views before dropping down to the valley for a tranquil stroll back along the **River Otter**.

3   3¼H   9.5 miles/15km   190m / 190m   4

Access by car: From **Exeter** follow the A30 towards **Honiton** then take the B3174 turning to **Ottery St Mary** and park near the bridge over the **River Otter**.

Ottery St Mary

One of the oldest towns in Devon, **Ottery St Mary** has several claims to fame. The parish bounds were determined in 1061 by Edward the Confessor and there have since been many royal associations. The poet Samuel Taylor Coleridge was born in **Ottery** in 1772 and its literary connections also extend to featuring in the works of Thackeray and, more recently, to a mention in the Harry Potter books as **Ottery St Catchpole**. The beautiful and renowned 14th century **St Mary's Church** crowns the town from above but **Ottery** is famous world-wide for its Tar Barrel Rolling. On November 5th flaming tar-soaked barrels are carried dramatically through the crowd-lined streets - juniors, then women and finally men, often generations of the same family, demonstrate their strength, fearlessness and prowess until the last barrel is proudly borne at midnight. It looks hair-raising and it is! A massive bonfire and funfair add to this unique attraction which draws crowds of thousands from all over the world.

We make our way to the western outskirts of the village to start the walk turning left onto a footpath heading south just before the **Otter Bridge** (Wp.1 0M) and keep left on a little embankment away from the river.

Just after a right bend on the dyke we turn left (Wp.2 3M) down some wooden sleeper steps and up under an ivy covered arch still following the path as we cross a footbridge (Wp.3 7M) into a field. Heading for a small gate into a second field at the top of the rise we bear right skirting trees on our right with the river meandering below. After 300yds we take

Ivy arch

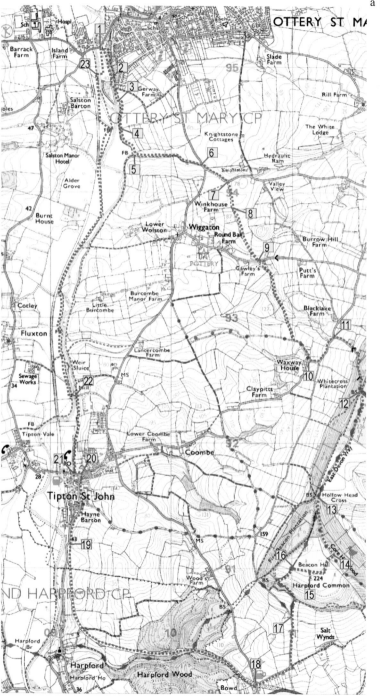

small gate on the right (Wp.4 13M) following the path heading down the through the trees to the flood plain, with the river oxbowing away from us. We follow the base of the embankment left and head for a wooden gate onto a broad track (Wp.5 17M) where we turn left (E) towards the wooded **East Hill** ridge. The track passes through a gate onto a road (Wp.6 24M) which we cross with a short right/left zigzag to a lane signed to 'Knightstone Manor' and then after 200yds we take a public footpath right through a gate (Wp.7 27M). We follow the footpath sign directing us south past a single tree in the middle of the field to a stile and some steps in the hedge opposite (Wp.8 32M) then, carrying straight on, we hug the hedge to our right with a green well rounded knoll on our left.

green knoll

Dropping into a valley we follow the path out onto a lane at the bottom of the field with farm buildings to our right (Wp.9 41M). We turn left at the lane then immediately right on a footpath, climbing gently through scrub and then into a remarkable landscaped woodland garden.

landscaped woodland garden

The path leads into fields and we turn left on an earthy track past **Little Waxway** to a lane and a cluster of houses with the impressive thatched **Waxway Farm** to the right (Wp.10 58M). Turning left on the lane we climb steadily with good views opening up over the **Otter** valley and the **East Hill** ridge rising on the right. After 300yds at **Blacklake Cross** (Wp.11 63M) we turn right tackling the escarpment head on, slogging steeply up the narrow lane to **White Cross** (Wp.12 72M) at the crest.

White Cross view

Getting our breath back we admire the fabulous views west from the wooded ridge with many Dartmoor *tors* clearly visible. We continue right from the road into the parking area then head (SSW) on a level broad stony track initially between the trees, later skirting the edge of the wooded area with views now opening up to our left with occasional glimpses of the sea. Carrying straight on at **Hollow Head Cross** (Wp.13 84M) we then fork left after 100yds still on a broad track into **Core Hill** beech wood, taking a footpath right as the trees end (Wp.14 90M). We now cut across open moorland on a broad track through the low heather and gorse, turning left on a short diversion to the trig point on **Beacon Hill** (Wp.15 95M) and enjoying the view to the coast. Returning to the main track we continue left reaching a T-junction with a stony track after 200yds (Wp.16 99M) and turn left to zigzag in the steep descent from the ridge through **Harpford Common**. Meeting a lane (Wp.17 107M) and exiting **Fire Beacon Hill Nature Reserve**, we continue straight down turning right at the T-junction below then emerging at a main road (Wp.18 115M). We turn left over a disused railway bridge then immediately right into a driveway, then right again through a gate down onto the course of the old railway track.

old railway track

River Otter

The line was originally owned by the **Sidmouth Railway Company** and at its peak in the 1930's operated 24 trains daily; it was closed in 1966 as part of the Beeching cuts. We follow the old track, now a permissive bridle path, for almost 1¼ miles through a wooded gorge, its sheltered cuttings lined with verdant ferns, before joining a lane (Wp.19 145M) and turning right to **Tipton St John**. At a T-junction in the centre of the village (Wp.20 152M) we go left towards the **Golden Lion** pub and bridge over the **River Otter** but, before reaching either, we turn right after 20yds on a narrow earthy track between houses (Wp.21 153M). Our way is alongside gardens following a small stream and gradually drawing closer to the river on the left. We join the river at an old dilapidated mill (Wp.22 164M) and cross via a sturdy footbridge to turn right and follow the river up-stream passing an impressive weir built to feed the mill.

After enjoying a two mile stroll along the river bank looking for kingfishers and dippers we approach **Ottery St Mary** and take a footbridge across the river (Wp.23 188M), turning left back to the footpath at the start of the walk (Wp.24 191M).

It's well worth having a pair of binoculars to hand for this very varied walk; the birdlife is fantastic, the cliffs are dramatic and the return along the **River Otter** is wonderfully tranquil. The walk starts at the mouth of the **Otter** and explores both banks of the estuary before heading north along the distinctive red cliffs of the **Jurassic Coast** taking in **Ladram Bay** and one of the highest points at 500ft on this section of the coast, **High Peak**.

Access by car: Lime Kiln long stay car park on the seafront in **Budleigh Salterton**, although expensive, usually has spaces.

Stroll: There and back from the car park along the **River Otter** as far as you fancy.
Shortcut: At Wp.7 turn left towards **Otterton** picking up the main route at Wp.13 in the village. Time 2 ¼hours; Distance 6.5m, 10.5km

With the sea behind us we set off (Wp.1 0M) aiming for the far end of the car park by the children's play area and cricket ground, taking the clearly signed coastal path to 'Sidmouth'. Birdlife abounds as we make our way past the new hide, the **Otter** estuary to our right and nature reserve wetlands to the left. Egrets, herons and a good variety of ducks and gulls distract us as we make our way to **White Bridge** (Wp.2 11M) and turn right to cross the river still following the coast path, this time towards **Ladram Bay**.

There's some free parking here but space is limited hence the recommendation to leave the car in **Budleigh**. We stroll on, ignoring a turning to the left, coming to **South Farm** driveway and a small gate on the right (Wp.3 13M) which leads us on a narrow earthy track heading south, back along the other side of the estuary once the site of medieval salt pans and giving rise to the town's name. With pretty glimpses of the sea, the shingle bank and **Budleigh Salterton** through the pine trees, we follow the path up to

the point where river and salt water mingle (Wp.4 26M) to turn left parallel with the sea along the edge of a grassy field. As we climb the first little rise we are treated to great views of the glittering water, a multitude of blues and greens and an impressive unshielded drop on the right -   children beware! Our walking is straightforward, gentle ups and downs, and all the people we meet greet us warmly; there's something very cheery about this stretch of coastline. Great pillars of red rock make excellent refuges for swooping gulls and **Big Picket Rock** stands out clearly ahead below the steep cliffs and wooded point of **High Peak**.

The **Jurassic Coast** stretches 95 miles from **Exmouth** in the west to **Old Harry's Rocks** near **Swanage**. It was declared a UNESCO World Heritage site in December 2001 being the first such site on the British mainland to be awarded such an accolade. The rocks along this stretch of the coast stem from 180 million years of the Earth's history with the distinctive red cliffs and pebble beds found from **Exmouth** to **Sidmouth** being the oldest, dating back to the *Triassic* period when the whole area was a landlocked arid desert bisected with wide meandering rivers. The famous **Budleigh Salterton** pebble beach is composed of hard quartzite once transported in the bed of one of these giant rivers. The action of Long Shore Drift ensures that the stones are carried great distances, even as far as Kent.

The path levels as we approach a dilapidated lookout above **Twopenny Loaf Rock** (Wp.5 53M) and we continue straight on, flanked by gorse to the right and flinty fields to the left. Ignoring a permitted path to **Otterton** (Wp.6 58M) we are shepherded through territory by ranks of small birds and skylarks, the hedges giving strong clues as to the prevailing wind direction, until we come to another shortcut to **Otterton** at a small wooden gate (Wp.7 67M). We follow the coastal path towards **Ladram Bay**, the caravan park and its leisure facilities quickly revealing themselves (not altogether attractively) on the hillside leading down to the roaring shingle beach shielded by its towering red cliffs. A kissing gate takes us close by the caravans and through a play area to come out at a thatched cottage (Wp.8 75M) where a diversion to the right invites us down to the beach, possibly for a laze and refreshment? Crossing the slipway we keep close to the cottage, still on the signed 'coast path', and wander past the restaurant building and play areas thankfully to emerge through a gate into fields. It's a steady uphill now, the tempting viewpoints on the right giving us a replay of our route and after about 12 minutes we strike out into

woods at a gate (Wp.9 87M). Cautionary notices regarding dogs and fire duly heeded, we welcome some shade for our continuing ascent. A passing walker blithely advised us that 'the worst is yet to come' and he was right, although an energetic climb to the High Peak trig point is optional! There are one or two narrow paths leading off to the right, choose any of them and scramble up to the top on slippery pine needles for some really fabulous views (Wp.10 95M). Returning to our broad earthy track we stroll on, easy level walking now, to a kissing gate and T-junction (Wp.11 101M) and take the public right-of-way to 'Bar's Lane, Otterton' to the left. We step out briskly on our wide track gently downhill, with lovely Devon countryside on our right, woodland on the left and pretty views ahead. Passing **Seaview Farm** (Wp.12 114M) and keeping right we pick up the lane, passing **Stantyway Road** on the left (Wp.13 124M), down to the pretty thatched cottages of **Otterton**. At **Fore Street** (Wp.14 127M) we turn left towards **Budleigh Salterton** - there are several opportunities for refreshment here; the **Kings Arms**, the shop and Post Office make a good start but **Otterton Mill** on the left, 'restaurant, gallery and crafts, bakery and food shop, artists' studios, working mill exhibition' is highly recommended. Past the mill and over the **River Otter** we spot our path to the left signed 'Budleigh Salterton' (Wp.15 134M) for a gorgeous, lazy meander alongside the river accompanied by ducks, wagtails, kingfishers and probably a few dogs intent on a good swim.

Resisting **Clamour Bridge** (Wp.16 148M), a small metal footbridge, we amble onwards crossing a *leat* by lovely daydream riverbanks coming to **White Bridge** again and retracing our steps to the car park (Wp.17 175M).

River Otter

16 Exploring Woodbury Castle and Five East Devon Commons

Much of the charm of Devon lies in the variety and diversity of the countryside. This walk visits five of the seven **East Devon Pebblebed Commons**, areas of increasingly rare lowland heath. The whole area is designated a site of special scientific interest and attracts visitors all the year round for walking, picnicking, observing fauna and flora and exploring the massive **Woodbury Castle** hill fort. The area is also used extensively but unobtrusively by the Royal Marines and is the site of their famous cross country course.

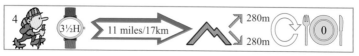

4 | (3½H)* | 11 miles/17km | 280m / 280m | 0

Access by car: From **Exeter** take the B3179 through **Woodbury** to **Four Firs** cross roads and turn left the on B3180 towards **Ottery St Mary** and the golf course. After approximately ¼ mile turn right into a car parking area just before the trees of **Woodbury Castle**.

Shortcut South Omitting **Dalditch Common** 14km 9miles 3 hours
At Wp.12 we continue straight on (SE) along the track, crossing a road after 200yds into **Wheathill Fire Point 4** car park (Wp.39). Strolling on in the same direction we follow the path through trees, ignoring a cross track and forking right at a split in the track past a small dilapidated building (Wp.40). Still heading SE we pass a path joining from the right then bear left between two grey metal poles (Wp.41) climbing gently (E) for 250yds where we turn left on a footpath (Wp.24) (N) to rejoin the main walk.

Shortcut North Omitting **Colaton Raleigh Common** 12km. 7.5miles 2hours 40min
At the main road in **Yettington** (Wp.27) we turn left towards **Exeter** for 600yds taking care on the fairly busy road, turning right on a bridleway (Wp.42) skirting round woods on the left then right. Following blue waymarks we continue straight ahead at a cross tracks (Wp.43) and turn left at a T-junction (Wp.44) climbing steadily up towards **Woodbury Castle** on a broad stony track. As we approach the Castle plantation we fork right (Wp.45) following the woods round on our left and rejoining the main walk at Wp.36 turning left back to the carpark (Wp.38).

leaving Wp.5

From the carpark (Wp.1 0M) we head back to the road and cross to a clearly marked bridleway (W) through trees and gorse away from **Woodbury Castle** soon reaching a T-junction (Wp.2 2M) and turning left. The path skirts the edge of the common up on our left with hedges and trees on the right bordering open fields. At a split in the path we fork left (Wp.3 8M) climbing away from the trees, with glorious views of the **Exe** estuary and hills beyond on our right as we make our way back to the road 100yds north of the **Four Firs** junction (Wp.4 12M). Crossing directly over the road we find a small track that swings right parallel to the road taking us down to the eastern arm of the junction which we cross into a carpark (Wp.5 14M).

We leave the carpark (SSE) climbing over a low metal barrier taking a stony vehicle track heading across **Bicton Common** towards a gap in the plantation on the skyline ahead. Ignoring a cross tracks as we approach the conifer wood we carry straight on then as we exit the wood the main path turns left and we continue downhill (SSE) on a small track littered with beautifully rounded pebbles towards a water filled gravel pit. As we approach the quarry, notices warn 'Danger Do Not Swim' (Wp.6 23M), not that the muddy red water looks very inviting!

We crunch along the edge of the workings then bear sharp left on a diversion round a newly fenced off quarry extension heading downhill (NE) to intersect another track (Wp.7 33M) where we turn right and climb out of the valley. On the crest of the hill we pass on the left one of the tunnel obstacles of the Royal Marine assault course (rather them than me!) then on into a clearing (Wp.8 36M) where we take the second broad gravel track on the right marked with pink and blue waymarks.

assault course

We drop down into a dip on a stony track then climb steadily on an old brick surface into a few conifers, then following the signs right we meet the quarry again and still following the blue waymarks step over a low barrier onto the road (Wp.9 44M).

quarry

Turning right then after 30yds left we enter **Upper Thorn Tree** car park (Wp.10 45M) to be confronted by a confusing array of exits - we choose one directly opposite our entrance point heading off between a willow and silver birch (Wp.11 46M). We snake through the bushes for 40yds turning left at a T-junction onto a signed footpath (SE) out onto the heathland, trees on the left and gorse and heather right. After 200yds at a cross tracks (Wp.12 49M) we turn right on a broad path onto the heath, continuing straight across another track then dropping down towards a reservoir in the wooded valley below. At the next junction (Wp.13 53M) we turn left still down towards the water and then go right at a small metalled lane (Wp.14 54M). After 100yds we take a left off the road (Wp.15 57M) into a carpark area which we exit (SE) on a footpath to **Squabmoor Reservoir**, making our way through gorse down a small valley to the water (Wp.16 60M). We follow along the side of the water, a beautiful tranquil area, to the dam (Wp.17 64M) at the southern end of the lake. Joining the vehicle access track swinging left and climbing out of the valley we drop (SE) to the settlement of **Dalditch**. We meet the road through **Dalditch** on a bend (Wp.18 75M) turning left passing the farm and just past **Dalditch Apiary** (Wp.19 77M) take a broad sunken track left gently up between steep banks. After 300yds we turn left at a cross tracks (Wp.20 81M) still steadily climbing and after a further 300yds (Wp.21 85M) we leave the track right onto an earthy footpath into woodland, immediately forking left past a holly bush on the right then climbing more steeply following waymark signs. The trees thin out and we make our way through gorse straight across two cross tracks then over a stile (Wp.22 90M) into a grassy field. Following the line of a hedge on our right we drop down to a stile in the corner of the field (Wp.23 94M) which takes us onto **Hayeswood Lane** (a *green lane*) where we turn left towards **Hayes Wood** ahead on the right. The deeply rutted lane leads us gently down between high hedges and at a footpath sign we turn right (Wp.24 99M) up into the dark conifer wood. A short climb then descent brings us through the trees where we do a right/left zigzag round a cottage past very vocal canine guardians, luckily safely locked away, then down the cottage access track to **Hayes Lane** (Wp.25 110M). From here it is well worth diverting 150yds left to view **Hayes Barton**, birthplace and home of Sir Walter Raleigh.

Hayes Barton

Sir Walter Raleigh was born in **Hayes Barton** in 1552 and became one of Queen Elizabeth's favourites most notably known for throwing his cloak down so that she could cross a puddle. He was not so lucky with her successor James, however, who had him beheaded in 1618.

Hayes Barton was built in about 1480 and is a typical Devon farmhouse. Originally the house would have been a basic rectangular layout, the wings and porch being added at a later date making the E shaped floor plan common at that time, thought to be developed as a compliment to Queen Elizabeth I. (N.B. The house is not open to the public).

To continue we cross directly over the road through a kissing gate onto a footpath (N) climbing the hill behind **Hayes Barton**, following the right-hand side of the field. A stile takes us up into the next field where we still follow the hedge on our right then drop down towards the houses of **Yettington**. A kissing gate (Wp.26 119M) takes us from the field onto a road where we turn right coming to an offset crossroads in the village. We turn right then left on a lane signed to **Colaton Raleigh** (WP.27 121M) for a pleasant stroll along a typical Devon lane with lush verdant banks, turning left at **Stowford Cross** (Wp.28 135M). We leave the lane after 300yds as it bends right (Wp.29 140M) carrying straight on along a bridleway into woods keeping right down to a small ford then straight on following the edge of the wood on our left and open fields right. Large 'Danger' signs (Wp.30 153M) warn us that we are near to a military firing range which we must not enter if the flags are flying so we turn right following waymarks into silver birch woodland skirting the eastern side of **Colaton Raleigh Common**. We keep left on the bridleway ignoring a right fork to **Kingston** (Wp.31 162M) still keeping to the edge of the common with patchwork fields and rolling hills on our right. At a low barrier and T-junction with a broad stony track (Wp.32 172M) we take a sharp left turn and head off uphill onto the heathland, a vast area of heather, gorse and occasional silver birch and open views south to the coast. Heading WSW we keep left at a fork and straight on at a cross tracks following pink waymarks (Wp.33 189M) making for the woods surrounding **Woodbury Castle** ahead. Passing a small copse of Scots pine on our right (Wp.34 195M) we go straight across a broad track staying with the pink waymarks up to a seat on the edge of the ancient fort (Wp.35 209M).

Woodbury Common

Woodbury Castle is a spectacular prehistoric hill fort built around 500-300BC at the highest point on the common, some 600ft above sea level. It commands the whole of the **Exe** estuary and must have been a formidable place to attack given its position and the very strong defences composed of two great ramparts separated by a ditch up to 20ft deep. It is believed to have been last used as a camp during the Napoleonic wars around 1800. Today the fort is defended by children undertaking mock battles and bikers taming the mountainous ditch.

Woodbury Castle

Our car lies directly ahead across the fort and can therefore be reached by either negotiating the massive earthwork defences or by taking a more sedate route around the outside. We choose the latter entering the wood and turning left along the side of the first earth bank, then follow the banks right (Wp.36 212M) and right again (Wp.37 214M) up into the carpark (Wp.38 216M).

The picturesque village of **Lustleigh** with its renowned inn and tea rooms is an ideal place from which to explore the wooded hills and deep valleys that surround the little community. We start the walk winding our way through the village past the cricket ground heading off to explore the impressive **Shaptor Rock** and tranquil woods on our way to **Hennock**. Our return route takes us past the old **Great Rock** 'Treacle Mines' then up to the **Tottiford** and **Trenchford** reservoirs before heading back via the restored **Kelly Mine** to **Lustleigh** and well earned refreshment.

| 4 | 4H | 10 miles/16km | | 350m / 350m | | 4 |

Access by car: leave **Bovey Tracey** on the A382 towards **Moretonhampstead** and turn left after 3 miles towards **Lustleigh**. Park on the street near the church.

Setting off from **Lustleigh** Church (Wp.1 0M) we make our way with **Primrose Cottage Tea Rooms** on our right down to the Gospel Hall taking a narrow lane alongside cottages to join the river as it surges under the disused railway bridge.

Past the village cricket ground on our left we reach another group of charming thatched cottages (Wp.2 4M) and a fork in the lane where we turn left alongside immaculate gardens up to a T-junction. We turn left and then 200yds further on reach a crossroads

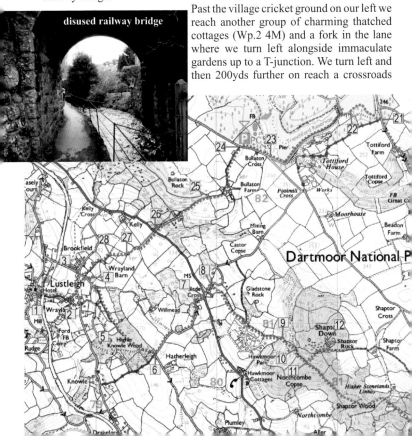

disused railway bridge

(Wp.3 7M) and take the no through road right; after 40yds the road splits (Wp.4 8M) and we keep straight on uphill following the footpath signed 'County Road near Hatherleigh'. The small access road ends after 100yds to become a narrow muddy path between hedges and banks littered with primroses. A gate (Wp.5 17M) takes us into the pretty **Higher Knowle Wood** owned by the Woodland Trust and after a level stroll keeping left at a fork we exit through a gate onto a lane (Wp.6 23M). Turning left we step out towards the wooded hill ahead reaching the main road at **Slade Cross** (Wp.7 30M) and go straight over to climb the narrow lane opposite. After about a minute we negotiate a stile onto a footpath right (Wp.8 31M) making our way along the side of the farm on the right. Woods cover the hillside on the left with open views over to the moor on the right as we come to a cross tracks and carry straight on keeping alongside the hedge on the right to the rear of the new houses at **Hawkmoor Park**. After a small wooden gate leading into rougher ground we step over a small stream and continue into conifers soon coming to a larger water course tumbling down the hillside in a cascade of waterfalls (Wp.9 44M). Crossing over we climb steeply up the hill ahead following waymarks alongside a moss covered stone wall on the right. At a broad track we carry straight on reaching a stile that takes us into **Shaptor Woods** (Wp.10 48M), a dramatic sign warning of the dangers that lie ahead!

We soon understand the nature of the hazard as we pass several fenced off areas marking the positions of old mine shafts

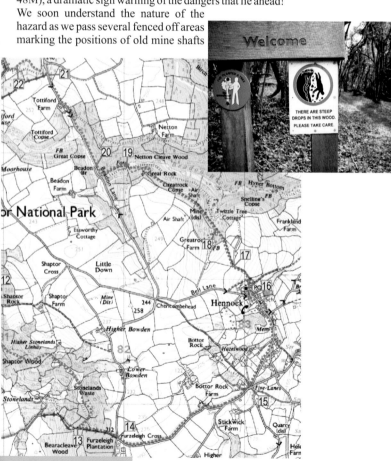

before coming to a fork in the track (Wp.11 50M). Rather than continuing straight we take a short diversion left climbing steadily to the viewpoint on **Shaptor Rock** (Wp.12 58M) - it's well worth the effort to see the fabulous vista of the **Bovey** valley and Dartmoor beyond.

We retrace our steps and turn left on the permitted path to ramble through the beautiful **Shaptor Wood**; the narrow path takes us down through the trees, wind damage causing us to divert around tree trunks blocking the way. After a mile we leave the woods at a gate (Wp.13 95M) from where we turn left on an broad earthy track lined with beech trees up to the road at **Furzeleigh Cross** (Wp.14 102M).

Shaptor Rock view

We head straight across at the junction taking the quiet lane to **Hennock** with views right over verdant Devon countryside towards **Chudleigh** nestling below **Haldon Hills**. At **Five Lanes** junction (actually seven ways if you count the access drives) (Wp.15 118M) we continue to **Hennock** passing the primary school and on up to the **Palk Arms** to the right (Wp.16 128M) and the lovely thatched village hall on the left. Our way takes us straight on along **Church Road** passing **St Mary's Church** then onto a track signed 'Beadon Bridge' which takes us right through a white gate onto a private driveway. After squeezing through a

beech lined track

tight kissing gate left (Wp.17 136M) we cross pasture exiting at another gate into woods and a sharp descent on an earthy path to a farmyard in the valley (Wp.18 142M). We take a concrete roadway right for 20yds then follow the signs left steeply uphill, heeding the notice not to stray from the path. Climbing up into the woods the evidence of old mining activity is plain to see; this is the site of **Great Rock Mine** known locally as the '**Treacle Mine**'. We traverse the side of the steep valley on our right passing between the huge boulders of **Great Rock** before winding our way down to the footbridge across **Beadon Brook** below(Wp.19 161M).

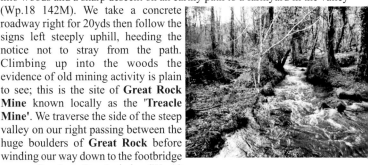

The Treacle Mines in the vicinity of **Hennock** and **Moretonhampstead** are more than a fiction dreamt up in a child's story book; they did exist mining a thick black treacle-like substance for more than a hundred years starting during the 19C. The molasses-like viscous liquid that oozed from the rocks was micaceous haematite (shiny ore) used in the manufacture of anti-corrosion paints, large quantities being required for the **Royal Navy** fleet. The

Kelly Mine

most famous, the **Great Rock Mine** just north of **Hennock**, was the last Dartmoor metal mine finally closing in 1969. The **Kelly Mine** near **Lustleigh** was shut down in 1951; the site is now managed by the **Kelly Mine Preservation Society** which meets every Sunday and organises restoration projects for the old mining machinery.

Over the brook our path bears left gently uphill with the stream rushing dramatically through rapids on the left and after 300yds we join a lane (Wp.20

Tottiford Reservoir

169M). Turning right we climb steadily through woods past **Tottiford Farm** and up to **Tottiford Reservoir** at the head of the valley (Wp.21 182M) and after making our way 10yds through the surrounding trees we join the path at the water's edge and turn left. At **Tottiford Dam** (Wp.22 188M) we turn left on the lane following the edge of **Trenchford Reservoir** then cross **Trenchford Dam** and bear right to **Bullaton Cross** (Wp.23 199M). Here we carry straight on towards **Moretonhampstead**.

After a short rise we take a footpath left signed 'County Road near Kelly' (Wp.24 202M) down a broad stony track diverting right as we approach farm buildings. We follow blue waymarks round the back of the farm then diagonally across a field to a gate leading into trees (Wp.25 208M). We follow the clearly marked path down through the woods joining the main road alongside the disused **Kelly Mine** (Wp.26 224M). Carefully crossing the road we take the footpath to **Lustleigh** across a field with the hedge on our right to a stile then after maintaining our direction for 100yds, we turn right over a well concealed ladder stile (Wp.27 229M). We head (W) across a small boggy field to a gap in the hedge opposite then bear left to the corner of the next field where duck boards help us across mud and onto a track (Wp.28 233M). This leads us back to the junction at Wp.4 at the beginning of the walk. Turning right then left we fork right past thatched cottages to retrace our steps to the church in **Lustleigh** and our car (Wp.29 244M).

It's just possible to resist the lure of the beautiful **River Teign** at **Steps Bridge** for this lovely countryside walk up and away in the hills. We climb out of the valley to discover the legendary giant granite outcrops of **Heltor** and **Blackingstone Rocks** then circle through gentle rolling upland farmland and wooded valleys to the nestling village of **Bridford** complete with inn and ancient church. The stroll back to **Steps Bridge** takes in glorious views across the **Teign** valley to **Haldon Hills** and beyond and then drops steeply back through woodland to our start.

3/4   3H   8 miles/13km   320m / 320m   2

Access by car: Steps Bridge lies ½ mile west of **Dunsford** on the B3212 **Exeter** to **Moretonhampstead** road. Park in the carpark opposite the Youth Hostel just west of the bridge.

Leaving the Steps Bridge carpark (Wp.1 0M), we turn left on the road downhill for 50yds then turn right into a small overflow car park (Wp.2 1M) just below the YHA. From the clearing we take the right-hand bridleway which steadily climbs up the wooded valley following a small stream initially on the right which we soon cross via a wooden footbridge. Still with the stream we progress up the valley crossing once again then, ignoring a left hand fork (Wp.3 10M), we then tackle a sharp incline alongside the rushing

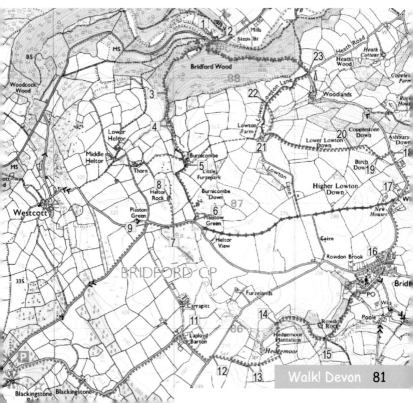

water. Signs indicate that we have left **Bridford Wood** as we continue on the bridleway through a gate following directions to **Burnicombe Farm** (Wp.4 16M). The path levels out through a rough meadow and we bend right across the stream using makeshift stepping stones to follow blue waymarks through a gate onto a muddy track to Burnicombe Farmyard. Seeing various signs pleading with walkers 'Please don't take our dogs on a walk with you send

Heltor Rock

them home!' we pass between the farm buildings and turn right on the bridlepath signed to the 'County Road' (Wp.5 22M) which climbs gently giving us our first glimpses of the majestic **Heltor Rock** towering above. We find that direct access to the tor from this direction is barred so we continue on our track along to the road and turn right (Wp.6 29M). After 200yds we are at last allowed towards **Heltor** over a small stile (Wp.7 31M) onto a permissive path directly to the rock (Wp.8 34M).

Well worth the wait and after a bit of a scramble the views are stunning looking over the south Devon coast, west into Dartmoor and north over the gentle Devon countryside. Hidden in the trees to the southwest lies our next destination, **Blackingstone Rock**.

The Legend of **Blackingstone** and **Heltor Rocks**
The story goes (although as with most Dartmoor legend there is more than one version) that once the Devil and King Arthur took up position, one at each vantage point, and hurled great rocks at each other. At last they could go on no longer - the impressive **Blackingstone Rock** is said to be King Arthur's final missile whilst the Devil could manage to heave no more than the still substantial **Heltor**.

Blackingstone Rock

Retracing our steps to the road we turn right and at **Plaston Green** crossroads (Wp.9 47M) we turn left following the lane for a mile as it undulates between verdant banks through woods and meadows. The closer we get to **Blackingstone Rock** the more majestic it becomes and we take the first opportunity to turn left (Wp.10 65M) from the lane onto a clearing towards the base of the rock-face from where there are many obvious tracks up to the top, a ladder providing the final challenging ascent for the more determined. Returning to Wp.10 we head east on the lane running away from the rock, initially through a conifer plantation then meandering peacefully between high Devon banks eventually discovering a cluster of very smart thatched cottages at **Laployd Barton** from where we take the lane right (Wp.11 85M).

We pass a splendidly restored ancient barn on the left, then after 300yds at a T-junction turn left and almost immediately find a small wooden gate and our footpath on the right (Wp.12 90M). The path follows the hedge on the left of the field dropping gently to an access gate in the corner (Wp.13 93M). A sign lets us know we're entering a private conservation area and we follow yellow waymarks through well managed pasture and woodland, turning

Laployd Barton Farm

right on a forestry track (Wp.14 101M) wandering down through woods alongside **Rookery Brook** below our third massive granite *tor* **Rowdon Rock** across the valley on the left. The track takes us through two gates and keeping left we join a small unmetalled lane (Wp.15 110M) where we turn left towards the white cluster of houses of **Bridford**. The **Bridford Inn** on the left offers well earned refreshment (if we have timed the walk correctly) but be warned - time slips away when sitting outside on this sunny, sheltered, south facing hillside! Alternatively **Bridford** church just past the inn offers a wealth of interest be it the magnificent Rood Screen or the fascinating bosses in the roof. The ancient motif of the three hares sharing just three ears whilst each appearing to have two is worth searching out.

From the inn we continue on the road going straight on past two turnings to the right and on reaching the next junction by a telephone box (Wp.16 123M) we bear right on **Neadon Lane** up and out of **Bridford**. The lane winds its way round **Higher Lowton Down** providing exceptional views of **Haldon Hills**, crowned by the white folly, **Lawrence Castle**, and more distant views over to east **Devon**.

Reputedly Devon's most sought after civil wedding venue, **Lawrence Castle** is perched high on **Haldon Hill** and stands in 5 acres of woodland in the heart of lovely **Devon** countryside some 6 miles from the cathedral city of **Exeter**. From its vantage-point, panoramic views extending to **Dartmoor**, **Exmoor**, the **South Hams** and the **Exe** valley and estuary can be enjoyed. On a really clear day even **the Isles of Purbeck** and **Portland Bill** in Dorset are visible. **Lawrence Castle**, also known as **Haldon Belvedere** is a Grade II* listed triangular tower originally built in 1788 by Sir Robert Palk as the centre piece to his vast estates and dedicated to the memory of Major-General Stringer Lawrence, the founder of the Indian army. Devon Historic Buildings Trust renovated the tower in 1994 and is ensuring its future by opening it to the public.

At **Windhill Gate** we take the left fork at a junction (Wp.17 132M) past **Higher Birchdown** on the left and then on to **Birchdown Farm** where we turn left onto a clearly marked diverted footpath 100yds after the farm entrance (Wp.18 138M). Yellow waymarks show our route as we skirt the back of the farm picking up the original track at a stile (Wp.19 141M) where we enter a large field and follow the fence line to an exit stile (Wp.20 146M).

The path narrows winding its way through high gorse before we join a fenced path then farm track down to **Lower Lowton Farm** (Wp.21 154M). Plenty of signs here keep us on the straight and narrow as we head towards **Steps Bridge** and **Burnicombe**, the footpath diversion taking us right, alongside a stream then swinging left to rejoin the original bridle path (Wp.22 159M) where we turn right. The stony bridleway flanked by low banks festooned with wild flowers emerges through a gate onto a lane (Wp.23 167M) where we turn left, not on the lane but along another track clearly signed 'Steps Bridge', passing a radio mast on the

orchids

right. After 100yds we enter **Bridford Wood** (NT) and, ignoring a right turn to **Steps Bridge**, follow the track (W) down through the wood to the clearing alongside the road (Wp.24 179M) and retrace our steps left back to the carpark (Wp.25 180M).

primroses

Feel like tramping into the wilds of central Dartmoor? Then this is the walk for you. Starting at the picturesque village of **Belstone** high up on the edge of the moor we venture south climbing gradually onto the Dartmoor plateau. **Hangingstone Hill** is our destination, a remote army lookout post from where the full extent of the north moor can be viewed. This is not a walk for a misty day or following prolonged rain as the terrain is quite remote and soft underfoot in places.

Safety Advice: please note that live firing frequently takes place on **Okehampton Range** it is imperative to check the firing times before undertaking this walk. See the safety notes in the Introduction.

Access by car: Leave the A30 from **Exeter** on the B3260 towards **Okehampton**. At the top of the slip road turn left and take the second left to **Belstone** and park near the pub, **The Tors**.

From **The Tors** (Wp.1 0M) we walk to the crossroads in the centre of the village (Wp2. 2M) by a telephone box and the **Old Telegraph Office**, turning left on a no-through road uphill. Passing a water treatment works on the right

Wp.6 boundstone

we continue to the end of the road at a gate onto the moor (Wp.3 7M) and carry straight on along a well-used broad stony track. The craggy rocks on **Belstone Tor** crown the hills to our left with **West Mill** and **Yes** *tors* dominating the skyline ahead as we crunch our way along the rough track. Passing to the right of the **Nine Stones** *circle* peeping above the gorse 50yds up from the track (Wp.4. 16M) we start to drop (SW) into the **East Okement River** valley coming to a fork in the track (Wp.5 26M). The path to the right leads down to the **Cullever Steps** ford, worth a visit, however we strike out left forking left again after 50yds then left yet again after a further 50yds by a trackside *boundstone* (Wp.6 28M) and take a grassy path following the line of **Irishman's Wall** up **Belstone Tor**.

Cullever Steps

Cullever Steps

Just up stream from the confluence of the **Black-a-ven Brook** and the **East Okement River** the military road from **Okehampton Camp** crosses both waterways in quick succession. Two bridges, two fords and two sets of stepping stones make up the crossing point known as **Cullever Steps** with the most intriguing feature being the paved fords which were constructed during the last century to enable heavy gun carriages to be pulled across the water without churning up the river beds. The large stone nearby marks the boundary between **Okehampton** and **Belstone** parishes and from it, looking east, the line of **Irishman's Wall** running over **Belstone Tor** can clearly be seen.

We swing right after 250yds onto a stony track, crossing the line of the wall and climbing steadily towards **Winter Tor** (Wp.7 37M) from where we look across the **East Okement** valley to **Rowtor**, **West Mill Tor** and **Yes Tor**. Continuing on the track we keep right at a fork (Wp.8 39M) heading south gently uphill, catching our first sight of **Oke Tor** ahead as the track levels out. We enter the firing range designated by a line of red and white poles (Wp.9 46M) and start to experience the true remoteness of Dartmoor's bald hills and tors as far as the eye can see. Level walking for ¾ mile on the grassy track brings us to **Oke Tor** (Wp.10 58M) with its army lookout point nestling to the south of the rock and commanding an unfettered view of the **East Okement** valley below. Still heading south we see our path ahead winding its way to the right of **Steeperton Tor** towards the small rectangular

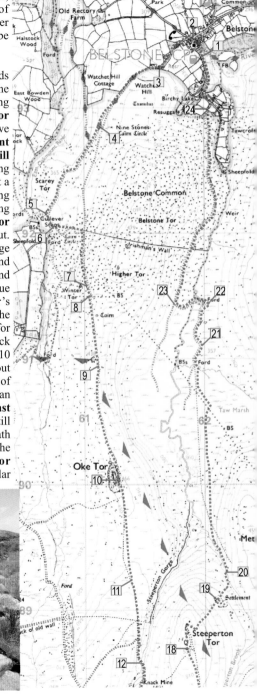

River Taw

nipple on the skyline - the summit of **Hangingstone Hill**. Our grassy path converges with a well-used stony track (Wp.11 67M) and we maintain our direction climbing gradually with **Steeperton Tor** above us on the left, then dropping to the site of **Knack Mine** and crossing the immature **River Taw** before it cuts into **Steeperton Gorge** (Wp.12 77M).

Continuing to follow the stony track we climb out of the valley and follow a rounded spur, the **Taw** valley on our right and **Steeperton Brook** on the left. We pass a small MOD concrete communications box (Wp.13 95M) on the right before we swing gently round to the left on the track as it snakes its way across the exposed moor towards the top of **Hangingstone Hill** (Wp.14 113M). An army lookout building and flag pole are the main features on the summit but there are stunning views all around. We truly are in the remote centre of the Dartmoor plateau.

Starting out on the return journey we head NNE on a grassy path in the direction of the massive rounded outline of **Cosdon Hill** on the skyline. Over the brow of **Hangingstone** we can see the jumbled rocks of **Wild Tor**, our next destination, in the dead ground ahead. A small *cairn*, which is in fact another MOD communications box, marks our path (Wp.15 128M) and soon after we reach **Wild Tor** (Wp.16 136M) where we change direction heading NNW towards **Steeperton Tor**. An indistinct grassy path takes us into the **Steeperton Brook** valley to a ford across the small stream (Wp.17 144M) where we can divert right to a tinner's hut before a steady climb to the commanding summit of **Steeperton Tor** (Wp.18 154M).

view from Steeperton Tor

crossing Steeperton Brook

Steeperton Taw from Taw Marsh

From the army lookout post we are able to survey the broad valley stretching north between **Belstone Tor** left and **Cosdon Hill** right and can just make out the path we plan to take across **Taw Marsh** below. From the *tor* we set off (NE) yomping along sheep tracks down into the steep-sided valley below, passing through the stone remains of an old settlement (Wp.19 161M) then on down to the brook. No formal crossing points are provided but there are plenty of boulders to help us across the rapid flowing water (Wp.20 169M).

The sheltered valley is idyllic, providing many spots to rest and while away the time before we set off again with the stream on our left following a narrow cutting taking us down onto **Taw Marsh**.

As the ground levels we head north on vehicle tracks across the short grass passing manholes associated with **Taw Marsh** water extraction system, joining a distinct track and crossing a dried up stream. At a track junction by a wired off enclosure we turn left (Wp.21 194M) which leads us to a shallow ford at a bend in the river (Wp.22 199M) from where we walk eastwards. After 300yds at a T-junction (Wp.23 203M) we turn right on a broad gravel track skirting around the base of **Belstone Tor** then dropping to leave the moor through a gate (Wp.24 222M). Finally we pick up a metalled road that zigzags through a group of houses and takes us back to the pub in **Belstone** village (Wp.25 229M).

Not only is **Bellever Tor** with its forested slopes an easily recognisable landmark from many locations in both north and south Dartmoor but it is also peppered with ancient *Bronze Age* sites. We start this walk from the hamlet of **Postbridge** and steadily climb the *tor* visiting several fascinating *stone circles*, *cists* and *stone rows* on the way - a breather at the summit allowing us to marvel at the all round view. Our return takes us down into the **East Dart** valley at **Laughter Hole** stepping stones then follows the river past **Bellever Bridge** on the way back to the famous clapper bridge at **Postbridge**.

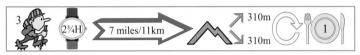

3   2¾H   7 miles/11km   310m / 310m   1

Access by car: Park in the car park at **Postbridge** on the B3212 **Princetown** to **Moretonhampstead** road.

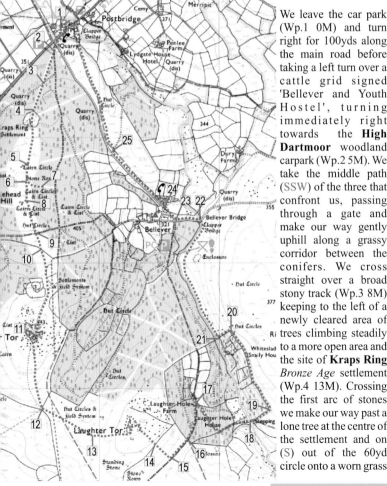

We leave the car park (Wp.1 0M) and turn right for 100yds along the main road before taking a left turn over a cattle grid signed 'Bellever and Youth Hostel', turning immediately right towards the **High Dartmoor** woodland carpark (Wp.2 5M). We take the middle path (SSW) of the three that confront us, passing through a gate and make our way gently uphill along a grassy corridor between the conifers. We cross straight over a broad stony track (Wp.3 8M) keeping to the left of a newly cleared area of trees climbing steadily to a more open area and the site of **Kraps Ring** *Bronze Age* settlement (Wp.4 13M). Crossing the first arc of stones we make our way past a lone tree at the centre of the settlement and on (S) out of the 60yd circle onto a worn grass track. After 500yds at a cross tracks (Wp.5 19M) as the ground levels out we divert right for 20yds to visit a small *stone circle*.

Retracing our steps to the cross tracks we continue (S) for 20yds to the top of

Cist Wp.7

Lakehead Hill coming to a distinct *stone row* running east, west across our path (Wp.6 23M). Bearing left on a broad grass-covered path we make another diversion crossing a track then over a stile into a small fenced off area protecting a very impressive *cist*. Six retaining stones encircle five supporting slabs and resting on these is a truly massive capstone. From there a row of about 11 stones runs downhill making this an awe inspiring site (Wp.7 25M). Well worth visiting!

tone circle

Returning to our original path we continue (S) and after 300yds (Wp.8 30M) divert 20yds right to see yet another ancient site consisting this time of two adjacent circles each about 10 yds across.

Many more sites are scattered in the vicinity of **Lakehead Hill** but we press on (S) along our track to **Bellever Tor**. Crossing straight over a broad open bridle track (Wp.9 36M) we yomp downhill on a narrow tussocky path aiming for the left of a boggy area, making for a gap in the stone wall (Wp.10 37M).

gorse and heather

Climbing gently now we admire the spectacular contrasting colours of the heather and gorse lining our track as we head up towards the granite rocks; the view from the top of **Bellever Tor** (Wp.11 47M) is surely one of the best on Dartmoor.

Descending from the trig point to the saddle between the two main granite lumps of the *tor* we take the track (S), picking our way through the rocky *clitter* then strolling down on a grassy path towards a wall and the edge of the plantation on our left. On reaching the wall (Wp.12 56M) we turn left through a gate on a distinct path across the moor heading just to the right of **Laughter Tor** and taking a left fork directly to the *tor* (Wp.13 71M). From the top a sheep fold dominates the view south with just beyond it a fine standing stone. We head (SE) on sheep tracks through gorse down towards a gap in the wall ahead (Wp.14 78M) then continue in the same direction until we intersect a broad path (Wp15 82M). Turning left, we pass through a gate (Wp.16 85M) signed 'Bellever' taking us into the **Bellever** plantation on a broad stony track edged with rowan trees and gorse. After 300 yds in front of a bungalow on our left we take a track to the right (Wp.17 89M) signed 'Sherril via Babney' (local spellings) almost doubling back on ourselves, then 10yds on fork right again on a earthy bridle path. We follow the path as it swings left downhill alongside the private grounds of **Laughter Hole House** with the hillside opposite glowing in autumn with gorse and heather. Passing through a gate with a sign reminding us we are on private land, we follow the path to **Laughter Hole Stepping Stones** (Wp.18 98M) and cross the river (long legs are a definite asset here) to a sheltered area of well cropped grass- an excellent place for a picnic.

Laughter Hole

We leave the signed footpath here and climb steeply uphill keeping as close to the wall on our left as possible diverting around the larger gorse bushes as necessary. As the climb moderates at a corner (Wp.19 104M), we turn left still following the wall now heading parallel with the river below. After 700yds we reach another corner (Wp.20 113M) and turn left again, scrambling steeply back down to the riverside (Wp.21 117M). A right turn now takes us alongside the **East Dart River**. With the trees of **Bellever** plantation on the opposite bank we stroll through a grassy open area, a popular playground for children, adults, dogs and wildlife, joining the road at **Bellever Bridge** (Wp.22 133M). We turn left on the road towards **Bellever** crossing the bridge and after 300yds, directly opposite the entrance to the woods (Wp.23 136M), we take a blue waymarked bridle path right which provides a shortcut into the village. Through a small wooden gate we join the road again (Wp.24 139M) and turn right passing a grey telephone box and gently climbing away from the settlement.

Looking out for a broad stony track on the right after 600yds (Wp.25 147M) we fork right, not on the track but on a grassy path almost parallel with the road heading directly back to **Postbridge**. We drop down through a gate to the famous old **Postbridge Clapper Bridge** then up onto the main road turning left past the **Post Office Stores** back to the carpark (Wp.26 163M).

Postbridge Clapper Bridge

Postbridge Clapper Bridge

There are about thirty clapper bridges in the Dartmoor area, the example at **Postbridge** being one of the finest. It's easily accessible, being very close to the main road, which may explain why it is one of **Dartmoor**'s most famous landmarks and 'must' for tourists. The bridge which possibly dates back to medieval times spans over 12m using four flat granite slabs estimated to weigh in total over 20 tons and has withstood the pressure associated with being totally submerged on at least three occasions. The bridge was lovingly and most recently restored in 1979 when it was noticed that one of the bridge piers was starting to lean precariously.

For a walk on wild Dartmoor with great views and some fabulous prehistory thrown in be tempted by this! Climbing onto **Stalldown Barrow** we have our first taste of *Bronze Age* antiquity with a splendid *stone row* and *circle*. Then an exhilarating tramp over sometimes unfriendly moorland brings us to Europe's, and possibly the world's, longest *stone row* running along **Erme Plains** and we finish with a relaxing stroll, the beautiful **River Erme** guiding us most of the way home.

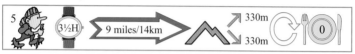

5 | (3½H) | 9 miles/14km | 330m / 330m | 0

Access by car: Leave **Ivybridge** (N) on the **Harford** road continuing left at **Harford** towards **Torr**. At **Torr** turn right and right again (NE) keeping left towards the moor at the **Yadsworthy Farm** turn. Continue through a gate and park at New Waste.

Stalldown Row

From the parking area at **New Waste** (Wp.1 0M) we ignore the concrete track leading to the water treatment works and instead take a footpath (N) to the moor alongside the boundary wall on the left. A leat runs along the right of the path and we cross it at a ford continuing straight up to a gate leading us onto the moor (Wp.2 8M). Turning right we follow the boundary wall making for the low rounded summit of **Stalldown Barrow** ahead and soon come to a prominent row of upright stones (Wp.3 23M) which lead us (N) for 500yds up the hill.

We find the tallest stone (Wp.4 33M) at the top of the row commanding a fantastic all round view with the bald and wild hills of south Dartmoor ahead, the spoil cone at **Redlake** providing the main landmark. Setting off (NNW) down a small spur into the saddle between **Stalldown Barrow** and **Stall Moor** we cross the marshy area around the lowest point (Wp.5 47M) and continue (NNW) starting to climb. Sheep tracks guide us through the tumpy grassland and, taking care not to twist an ankle, we tramp parallel to **Bledge Brook** in the valley to our right catching glimpses of **Plymouth Sound** between the hills on

Redlake Cone

our left. As the ground levels near the head of **Blatchford** valley (Wp.6 76M) we turn right (NE) directly towards the prominent **Redlake** cone on the skyline, cutting across the top of the valley (Wp.7 83M).

There's no shelter on this part of the moor and the walking is hard going, with long grass hiding treacherous holes in the boggy peat. However, after 800yds (Wp.8 96M) we begin our descent (E) into the **Erme** valley with the

River Erme

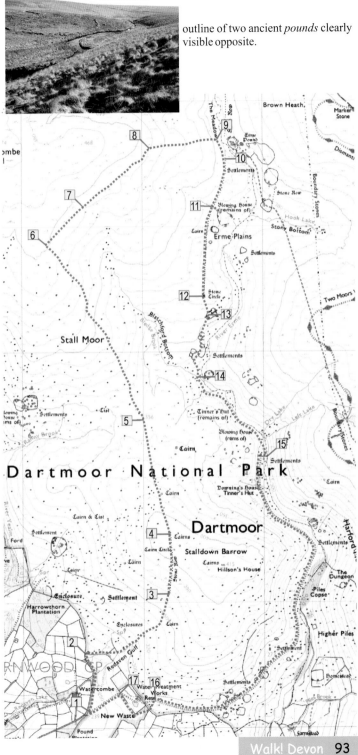

outline of two ancient *pounds* clearly
visible opposite.

The **Upper Erme Valley**

A magnificent collection of *Bronze Age* remains are to be found on the slopes of the **Erme** valley as the **River Erme** descends from remote moorland towards **Ivybridge**. The famous **Erme Stone Row** makes its way northwards across **Erme Plains** firstly on the western slopes of the valley and then on up to **Green Hill** on the east side; the row is typical in its N/S alignment but very unusual in that it is also kinked. Consisting originally of more than 1000 stones it is terminated by a burial *cairn* on **Green Hill** to the north and by a *cairn* enclosed by a *stone circle* of about 25 stones to the south, this *circle* being known as **The Dancers**. Legend has it that young folk were turned to stone to pay for the sin of dancing on a Sunday, a story replicated elsewhere on Dartmoor, for example at the **Nine Maidens** near **Belstone Tor**. The purpose of the *row* is unknown although it is thought likely to have ceremonial significance. The remains of four impressive *pounds* and associated *hut circles* are clearly visible on the eastern slopes of the valley, the largest and northernmost one being close to the point where the *stone row* crosses the **Erme** - clearly quite a substantial settlement.

We head (E) down towards the left-most *pound* soon seeing the river meandering below in the valley (Wp.9 107M). The **Stall Moor** *stone row* crosses the river in this vicinity but is very indistinct; however, it is just possible to spot the line of stones heading northwards up **Green Hill**. We turn right contouring the side of the valley about 100 yds up from the river and intersect the *stone row* (Wp.10 112M) then walk (S) with the line of small stones. Bearing right we climb steadily following a beaten track alongside the line of the stones, some sections being more distinct than others. Dropping into a deep gulley, a perfect picnic spot (Wp.11 119M) we strike out with the stones marching relentlessly across the moor, the river meandering in the

Erme Valley hut circle

valley on the left. After ½ mile 'The Dancers' *stone circle* marks the end of the row (Wp.12 131M) and looking back we can see the line extending to the horizon with outlines of settlements on the hillside across the valley on the right.

We continue (S) heading closer to the **River Erme** as it bends towards us, passing on the way another ancient *pound* enclosing a cluster of *hut circles* (Wp.13 135M) then dropping down to an area of old tin workings by the riverside. We follow the course of the river as it winds its way south and make our way on boulders across **Bledge Brook** (Wp.14 145M) before bearing SE past more tin workings still enjoying the babbling river on the left. Passing the twin clefts, **Dry** and **Left Lake** as they cut their way down the hillside opposite we track the river to a small lake, dam and concrete buildings (Wp.15 159M). The access road here makes for easy walking and we step out along the valley with views over **Ivybridge** to the coast opening up ahead. The path swings right climbing from the valley then dropping us gently down to **New Waste** water treatment works (Wp.16 201M). As we approach the works a waymark leads us left along the boundary then right through a gate and right again as we make our way around the fenced and wooded area. Joining a concrete track on the far side (Wp.17 208M) we turn left striding out down to the car park below (Wp.18 211M).

No walking book of Devon would be complete without a route featuring the famous **Haytor Rocks** -undoubtedly one of the most well known landmarks on Dartmoor. We begin our excursion from the pretty village of **Ilsington** and make our way up onto the moor with its expansive views at **Black Hill**. Taking in some interesting industrial archaeology at **Haytor Quarries** we finally achieve the summit at **Haytor Rocks** with its fabulous all round panorama - this has to be a walking highpoint in all senses! We reluctantly descend from the moor to return to our start through charming country tracks and lanes brimming with wild flowers and luscious foliage.

Access by car: Take the A38 from **Exeter** towards **Plymouth** and at the **Drum Bridge** A382 junction take the third exit signed 'Ilsington'. After 500yds turn right and follow the road for 2miles to **Ilsington** parking on the road in the vicinity of **St Michaels Church**.

Lych Gate

We start the walk from outside the **Carpenters Arms** pub (Wp.1 0M) taking the path alongside the pub into the churchyard and turning left past the church out onto the road via the magnificent west Lych-gate.

From the gate we turn right then left at the T-junction heading out towards **Haytor** reaching **Vicarage Cross** after 100yds (Wp.2 2M) and taking the right turn on a narrow lane signed 'Trumpeter'. The small hamlet is reached after 500yds where we bend right past cottages then, just past the last cottage as the road swings right, we continue straight on a no-through-road (Wp.3 11M) signed 'Smallacombe Farm'.

The lane gently climbs between high hedges and fields to the farmyard alive with a variety of hens, ducks and guinea fowl happily scratching around. We make our way through the farm buildings crossing a small ford and up to a cross tracks (Wp.4 19M) where we turn left on a bridleway passing through a gate then immediately right on a signed footpath to the moor. Extensive views down to the coast at **Teignmouth** open up on the right as we climb the muddy track which soon turns into an access lane at a couple of cottages on the left and levels out as we reach the drive to **Shotts House**. With a right/left dogleg and then

Smallacombe

through a gate we clamber up a bank onto the main **Haytor** road (Wp.5 28M) which we cross taking the small muddy track ahead then turning right parallel to the road on a wider grassy track. After 100yds, opposite the **Green Lane** road junction, we take a sharp left turn to start the climb onto **Haytor Down** picking our way through heather and gorse on a well used peaty path.

The imposing silhouette of **Haytor Rocks** dominates the view (SW) as we make our way up to a road ahead (Wp.6 48M). Ponies and sheep watch lazily as we cross into a parking area from where we bear right (NW) on a narrow path heading for a small boundary stone visible on the near skyline. Below us on the right **Yarner Wood** and **Trendlebere Down** lead our gaze down into the steep **Bovey** valley with **Lustleigh Cleave** on the far side. We take a short diversion right from the path to the boundary stone inscribed 'Old Jack' (Wp.7 54M) which is one of a series of stones erected by the Duke of

Haytor Rocks

Somerset around his land in 1853. Rejoining the path we continue soon seeing the next boundary stone in the series, **Victoria** (Wp.8 59M) from where we contour around the hillside then climb steadily to the **Black Hill** cairn (Wp.9 71M).

Black Hill

From this eastern edge of the moor we enjoy excellent views of beautiful Devon countryside, **Haytor** still dominating our view south and we set off from **Black Hill** directly towards the rocks on a wide track passing a second cairn (Wp.10 76M). We continue south selecting anyone of many paths cutting their way through the heather down to the **Granite Tramway** in the valley below **Haytor** and follow the tramway left (E).

Haytor Tramway 'Points'

Haytor Granite Tramway
The **Haytor Tramway**, built in 1820 by George Templer, was used for 10 years to carry stone, some for the new **London Bridge**, down to the **Stover Canal** 8 ½ miles away at **Ventiford**. The tramway is constructed from granite setts with a flange cut into them to hold the iron shod tram wheels; remarkably, granite points have been carved to allow branch lines to join with the main track. The stone was carried on trucks by gravity downhill 1300ft and horses were used to return the empty trucks back to the quarry.

Where a branch line joins the main track at a set of stone points (Wp.11 90M) we take the branch gently curving left towards the most easterly of the rocky spoil heaps marking the position of **Haytor Quarries**. Adjacent to the heap (Wp.12 94M) we turn right on a grassy path climbing up to the quarry with a small stile leading us on a stony path into the sheltered enclosure - an excellent place for a picnic. Skirting the edge of the small lake we search for its elusive goldfish before exiting at gate (Wp.13 100M) and turning right for the steep climb to **Haytor Rocks** (Wp.14 107M). It's always worth spending a few moments here exploring and climbing the outcrops, wondering at the extensive views whilst being entertained by others rock climbing, flying kites and playing hide and seek. We leave the rocks not towards the DNPA Information Centre but south down the well worn grassy track to the road and higher car park clearly visible below (Wp.15 111M) then, over the road, we take a track on the right of the carpark (S) leading alongside the shallow valley on the right. Reaching a stone wall (Wp.16 121M) just before **Bag Tor** we turn left (E) on a path alongside the wall and continue down through disused mine workings to the access track to and from the moor (Wp.17 133M). Our way runs along field boundaries between high Devon banks then drops steeply through conifers into a deep valley with a clapper bridge and ford across a small stream (Wp.18 141M). Over the stream we head out on a broad track past a newly planted wood meeting a lane (Wp.19 145M) where we turn right.

We carry straight on at **Birchanger** and **Sigford Crosses** then bear right at **Swinepark Cross** to follow the lane down to **Five Cross** (Wp.20 162M). Here we turn sharply left taking the well rutted muddy *green lane* squeezed between high hedges. At a cross tracks (Wp.21 170M)we turn left (N) back towards **Ilsington** soon dropping steeply down the notorious **Simms Hill** before climbing up to the village and taking the first turning right back to the **Carpenters Arms** and our car (Wp.22 186M).

Simms Hill at **Ilsington** is one of the most severe hill climbs featured in the Motor Cycling Club's annual Exeter Trial which takes place over two days early in January. The trial has been a regular event since 1910 and involves motorcycles and cars attempting to complete the route which includes a series of ferocious hills. **Simms Hill** was introduced into the trial in 1933 and is regarded by some as the most challenging - it's great fun to watch the intrepid crews bouncing and scrambling their way up (and all too often down) the rough, steep incline in their often interestingly customized transport.

The path between **St Marychurch** and **Shaldon** is one of the most strenuous sections of the South West Coastal Path so be prepared for some huffing and puffing up those headlands and some knee-crunching descents. Sounds uncomfortable? But it's well worth it - and of course a steady pace and some pleasant resting spots make all the difference for this kind of walking. So we heartily recommend this beautiful linear route which offers a pleasant bus ride, views of intriguing coves and a stunning coastline, a touch of industrial history and all this in the context of lush vegetation and, in springtime, a profusion of blossom and wildflowers.

3 | 2¼H | 5 miles/8.5km | 300m / 370m | 3

Access: Park in the **Shaldon** long stay pay-and-display car park at the top of the hill by **The Ness**. Allow 10-15 minutes for the estuary-side walk back into **Shaldon** to take the No. 85 bus to **St Marychurch** at the stop by the school near the **Teign Bridge**. As **St. Marychurch** golf course is passed on the left, prepare to alight in the centre just after the traffic lights at the **United Reform Church**. A five minute walk retraces the bus route back past the car park to the small roundabout, the golf course and **Petitor Road**.

The walk starts at **Petitor Road** (Wp.1 0M), a no-through road leading down to the coast along the southern side of the golf course. The lane ends at metal gates which take us onto a grassy area overlooking the sea (Wp.2 4M) where we turn left and drop down steps into a small valley skirting the edge of the course. Following the coastal path signs we turn right and right again (Wp.3 13M) zigzagging through woods down the cliff, then bear left levelling out and along the top of **Shag Cliff**.

Wire fencing protects us on the right as we look down on sheer red cliffs; shags, or are they cormorants, circle below protecting their nesting sites on ledges (to tell the difference cormorants, unlike shags, have a white throat and they're the ones that perch with open wings airing their arm pits). A steady ascent brings us above **Smuggler's Hole** overlooking **Watcombe Beach**, where a path joins from the left (Wp.4 23M) and we continue ahead swinging right and down into the cove. A tarmac track (Wp.5 27M) runs right down to the beach with an optimistic promise of a beach café and places to rest but we turn left then right after 20yds climbing steadily in woodland.

The **Valley of the Rocks** (Wp.6 31M) comes next as something of a surprise, an old quarry hidden in the trees which

Valley of the Rocks

produced red clay used in the manufacture of famous **Watcombe** terracotta ware.

Watcombe Pottery

In 1869 the owner of **Watcombe House**, Mr G J Allen, realized that the red clay, unique to this part of South Devon and abundant on his land, would work well for manufacturing the increasingly popular terracotta ware of the time and so set up the Watcombe Terracotta Clay Co. After initially selling the clay elsewhere, a pottery was set up in situ to produce the fashionable Watcombe collection, the items becoming even more of a 'must-have' when in 1873 Queen Victoria accepted a pair of Watcombe water bottles as a birthday present from Baroness Burdett Coutts. Christopher Dresser (1834-1904), one of the most successful designers of his time (he worked with both Minton and

Wedgewood) inspired pieces of Watcombe pottery, his signature being an assurance of 'good taste'. Watcombe Pottery is still available - just take a look on eBay!

The site now makes a mysterious and interesting playground for visitors. In the valley we bear right and climbing steeply we come to a junction where we turn right towards the coast (Wp.7 36M). This part of the path is common to the **John Musgrave Heritage Trail**, a new 35 mile path from

Cowslips

Blackthorn

Maidencombe to **Brixham** opened in March 2006 in memory of John Musgrave, former chairman of the South Devon Ramblers. The sheltered downhill trail is lined with primroses and bluebells with the occasional clump of cowslips in the meadow, an absolute delight during springtime!

Steps take us up into woodland and, hurrah, at last a level stretch. At a junction (Wp.8 49M) we turn right then immediately left over a stile into open fields signed as 'conservation land'. The well worn path follows a contouring route across the rolling hillside terminating at a second stile which takes us left back onto the coastal path (Wp.9 55M) and a steady descent beside windswept blackthorn hedges to the nestling settlement of **Maidencombe**. Toilets, overflowing waste bins and a carpark spoil the idyllic setting as we join the lane to the beach (Wp.10 60M) and turn left through the carpark up to the village. Happily our first impressions are soon forgotten as we come across the village pub **The Thatched Tavern** a very welcome refreshment stop - almost sub-tropical (Wp.11 63M).

Thatched Tavern

We pick up the coastal path (N) by retracing our steps from the pub downhill to the carpark entrance and taking the track on the left passing **Maidencombe Cottage;** for the sharp-eyed a waymark will be found hidden in the undergrowth on the corner. The track starts as an access drive to a few well hidden **Maidencombe** houses but soon turns into a path as it bears left along the side of **Windsong**'s garden and then continues on the cliff, edged with thick windswept hedges to the right and rolling fields on the left. The path is seldom level and we embark on a stiff climb up to the headland above **Mackerel Cove** (Wp.12 77M) from where we get fine views north along the coast to **Teignmouth** and

waypoint 15

beyond to the **Parson and Clerk** rock by **Dawlish**. We ignore the left turn here up to the main road, staying on the coastal path as it descends towards **Herring Cove**, passing another path left to the road above (Wp.13 87M) and then over a stile into another conservation area (oh that we were conserving height rather than nature!) We embark on yet another steep push barely finding the inclination to admire the abundance of violets and primroses clinging to the hillside. Over the next stile (Wp.14 92M) we welcome the respite of a small dip and then we're off again up steps, a stile, then more steps to the headland (Wp.15 97M) from where we get fine views south towards **Torquay.** The challenging terrain north is hidden from view by trees which is probably for the best.

Steep downhill now, just as hard on the legs as going up but at least for this section an alternative slalom course zigzags down alongside the uneven steps. We continue through rough woodland with the sea thundering below then exit at a kissing gate and follow round the right-hand edge of a grassy field hugging the cliff top climb a verdant, south facing slope up near the road. A kissing gate (Wp.16 110M) takes us past a sign indicating 'unstable cliffs' then down steps through vivid gorse bushes before climbing steeply at the back of grand design houses nestling in **Labrador Bay** up onto the road (Wp.17 121M). Turning right we have a short section alongside the road before going right again through a gate into a field (Wp.18 123M) and up to **Bundle Head**, overlooking **Shaldon Golf Course** with magnificent views of the **Teign Estuary**, **Teignmouth** and coast up to **Dawlish** with the Brunel railway hugging the undercliff. Our path takes us along the cliff top and for a stroll beside the golf course before veering right at the 17th Tee (Wp.19 136M) down steps onto a broad sunken track. Somewhat alarmingly, blood-curdling cries from the **Shaldon Wildlife Trust** greet us as we turn left from the track, but happily we are able to retreat to the safety of our car (Wp.20 140M).

A pretty bus ride from **Totnes,** this linear walk starts at **Marldon**, famous for its Apple Pie Fair held at the end of July each year. We then explore the gently rolling Devon countryside taking in the imposing and mysterious **Compton** and **Berry Pomeroy** castles on the way. With the abundance of *green lanes* making easy walking and several opportunities for historical interest and refreshment, this excursion provides a relaxing and fascinating day out.

3 | 3 H | 9 miles/14km | 250m / 370m | 4

Marldon Church

Access : Park in Totnes - the well sign-posted car park by **Steamer Quay** is very suitable. Walk to the Number 111 bus stop opposite the R**oyal Seven Stars Hotel** by the Memorial roundabout on the west side of the **Totnes** bridge over the **River Dart**. If there's time, it is well worth visiting the Tourist Information Office situated in the **Old Mill** a few yards up from the bus stop. Take the Bus to **Marldon Primary School**.

From the bus stop at **Marldon Primary School** (Wp.1 0M) we walk (N) downhill to **Kiln Crossroads** and then bear left on the **Ipplepen Road** climbing gradually and overlooking **Marldon Church** in the valley on our right.

At a sign for 'Church Hill' (Wp.2 4M) we turn sharp right downhill through some of **Marldon**'s older houses, forking left at the **Old School House** dating from Victorian times, past the 13C Church to join a lane (Wp.3 8M) where we turn left towards the charming 15C **Church House Inn.** We follow the lane turning left at the next T-junction (Wp.4 14M) towards **Compton** for a watchful stroll along this country road, being vigilant for the occasional passing car. After ½ mile we arrive at the **Castle Barton** restaurant on the right offering a range of refreshments, quickly followed by the imposing **Compton Castle** entrance on the left.

Compton Castle, built in 1340, has been home for most of the last 600 years to the Gilbert family closely related to Sir Walter Raleigh who was famed for spearheading the colonial expansion in North America during Elizabethan times. The house is a grand example of a fortified country mansion built to withstand attack from marauding French raiding parties from which there was a real threat during the reign of Henry VIII. The splendid house and grounds are now owned by the National Trust currently open to the public between April and October on Monday, Wednesday and Thursday but - don't get caught out, it's closed at lunchtime.

Continuing along the road past the castle for a further ½ mile we turn left at **Comptonpool Cross** (Wp.5 34M) onto **Windthorn Lane**, a rough unmetalled track gently climbing between high banks bedecked with masses of lush wild flowers; our stroll relaxed now, with only robins interested in our progress as they escort us between territories. The lane takes us to **Windthorn Cross** (Wp.6 48M) where we go left on **Ipplepen Road** for 500yds, turning right onto a rough track, **Aptor Lane** (Wp.7 56M), opposite the **Torbay and District Radio Flying Club**. We follow the track left past two gates on a slight incline and then descend gradually to the small settlement of **Aptor** where we continue forward until we meet a lane (Wp.8 70M) which we cross onto a public bridleway.

We amble gently down between fields and bluebell and wild garlic woodlands crossing under a power line, always keeping to the path and ignoring the footpath joining on the left from **Marldon**. Following the rough lane right towards **Afton** we use a wooden plank bridge to cross a small stream and soon

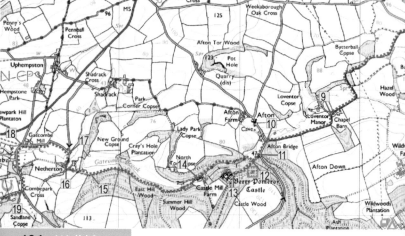

come to **Chapel Cottage**, part of the **Loventor Manor** settlement (Wp.9 86M). Keeping round to the left past a pink rendered cottage and guided by the blue waymarks of the **John Musgrave Heritage Trail** we step out on the road to **Afton Bridge** (Wp.10 95M). We turn left with the ruins of **Berry Pomeroy Castle** on the hill ahead and after 100yds, as the road bends left, we continue forward on a narrow no through road towards **Totnes** (Wp.11 96M). A closer look at **Berry Pomeroy Castle** is on the cards here so after a further 100yds we take a short detour left through a kissing gate (Wp.12 97M) and climb on a narrow track up to the castle (Wp.13 101M).

Berry Pomeroy Castle is reputedly the most haunted castle in Britain giving rise to numerous legends and experiences of strange lights and noises. The most common tales relate to sightings of a White Lady and a Blue Lady both being the apparitions of young women who have met untimely deaths within the walls. The Pomeroy family was given the lands around the present castle by  William the Conqueror in recognition of support given during the Norman invasion. The castle with its Norman gatehouse was built during the late 13C with mansion houses built at later stages within the confines of the grounds. Since 1977 the castle has been in the care of English Heritage; the grounds make a fine place for a refreshment stop.

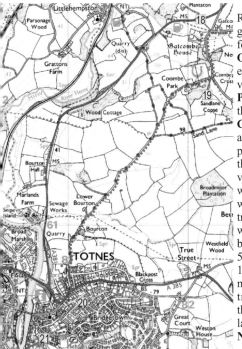

Retracing our steps to the kissing gate at Wp.12 we turn left and follow the track right, crossing **Gatcombe Brook** and skirting the edge of a small pond with a fine view of the outer defences of **Pomeroy Castle** atop the cliff on the left. After 500yds we reach **Castle Mill Farm** (Wp.14 109M) and fork left on the permissive path to **Netherton** ambling down through pasture into a small valley, crossing a stream before we join an earthy track into a wooded tunnel. Following the track we trace the edge of the wood with **Gatcombe Brook** below on the right until we reach a 5-bar wooden gate (Wp.15 121M). Through the gate into the meadow, we keep to the well trodden path downhill then through another gate out on to a lane at the small settlement of **Netherton** (Wp.16 123M).

Turning right we follow the lane past a group of farm cottages across a small stone bridge then at a junction by **Netherton Cottage** (Wp.17 124M) we turn left between high hedges alive with chiff-chaffs. At the next junction by **Gatcombe Mill** (Wp.18 129M) we turn left again, once more crossing **Gatcombe Brook**, then on past the grand **Gatcombe House** before climbing out of the valley. A wooden signpost pointing right along **Bourton Lane** to 'Coombe Park Equestrian Centre' (Wp.19 134M) indicates our next turn, taking us uphill past the Equestrian Centre where the lane gives way to a stony track marked by waypoints leading over the top of the hill. With **Totnes**

Steamer Quay

clearly visible ahead nestling in the next valley we follow the broad track (SW) passing through **Bourton** where we join a lane that takes us down onto the main A385 as it enters the town (Wp.20 163M). Turning right and crossing over the road we fork left **St Johns Church** and then go left just before **Totnes Bridge**, following signs to the carpark at **Steamer Quay** (Wp.21 171M).

This linear hike through a flowing landscape has a wealth of different views and offers a welcome alternative to the strenuous coastpath between **Brixham** and **Kingswear**; following part of the way-marked **John Musgrave** trail to **Greenway**, we connect with the **Dart Valley** trail to **Kingswear**.

From **Brixham's** busy fishing port we take the coastpath towards **Torbay** before heading inland, winding through woods to **Churston** village, then up a *green lane* into pastures with extensive rural views to **Dartmoor's** southern edge. From a spectacular viewpoint overlooking the **Dart** estuary we can visit Agatha Christie's secluded summer retreat at **Greenway**, before meandering down through mature woods above the **River Dart** to the tidal shore and a final relaxing stroll to **Kingswear**. The seasonal ferry which plies the river between **Dartmouth** and **Greenway** supports two appealing shorter walks.

Shorter walk A: Walk to Wp.7 then down to **Greenway Quay** for a seasonal ferry to **Dartmouth** 5 miles/8km A150m/D150m
Shorter Walk B: catch a seasonal ferry from **Dartmouth** to **Greenway Quay**. Follow signs for **Kingswear** uphill to join the walk at Wp.7. 5 miles/8km A170m/D170m
Walk Detour to **Greenway** gardens; ½ mile each way from Wp.7 20M

Public transport: Stagecoach bus Nos. 22 and 24 between **Brixham** and **Kingswear**. Stagecoach bus No.12 between **Newton Abbot** and **Brixham**.
Access by car: there are several car parks in **Brixham** which lies at the southern end of **Torbay** on the A3022.

In 1688 William of Orange landed at **Brixham** harbour to start his invasion of England; facing seawards on The Strand beside his statue (Wp.1 0M) (SX 926562), we go left along the quay side past an obelisk locating the actual landing spot. Keeping left in front of the Harbour Office between a red sea mine and colourful wall mosaic we pick up signs for 'Battery Point' strolling on a tarmac path to the outer harbour and enjoying sweeping views of **Torbay**. Beyond **Oxen Cove** car park we stay

Brixham harbour

beside the sea to the end of a concrete wall where we climb steps to Battery Point and the remnants of a WW11 gun emplacement. Going straight across a grass sward towards the cove, we curve inland, leaving the tarmac on an earth path, jinking right through a gap in a wall then left to the top of the beach.

At the toilets (Wp.2 16M) we climb inland up a tarmac lane signed 'Churston Cove', and turn right at a T-junction between holiday chalets along the

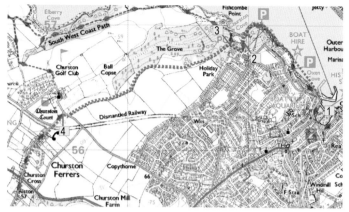

coastpath for 'Churston Ferrers'; going through a kissing gate into woodland we immediately bear left for 'Greenway' (Wp.3 19M). Our gently ascending broad path meanders through The Grove, a well used area of mature trees and large clearings, then after two stone pillars continues between dry stone walls and hedgerows to a stile and lane. We now turn right for 100 yards to a road junction and 'Churston' sign (Wp.4 38M); to visit **Churston** Church and/or public house go straight on along the lane for five minutes and return to this point. Our route bears left under a railway bridge and through **Fenners Green** passing a row of seven identical houses with red porches; just beyond them are cottages with railings across the doors, allegedly installed by a lady of the manor so that residents couldn't watch her pass by!

At the end of the lane, carefully crossing the main Paignton to Brixham A3022 road into Alston Lane, we head past Alston Farm's holiday accommodation to

rolling South Hams fields

join a *green lane* on our left (53M); following the **John Musgrave** trail marker we gradually climb between fields, taking time to look back over the broad sweep of **Torbay**. Going left for a few paces along a road (65M) we cross over and climb a stile on our right to be greeted with fabulous views across rolling **South Hams** fields to **Dartmoor's** unmistakeable southern tors. Striding across a field for 'Greenway' and over a stile, we bear slightly left along the contour, crossing the head of a valley then swinging right over a stile onto a path. Now turning right we crest the summit with fine views down **Galmpton Creek** to the **River Dart** and continue along field edges to a gate and path junction (Wp.5 82M) just before a small group of houses at **Higher Greenway**. Our eventual route is left along a 'Permissive path to Kingswear', but we urge you to continue ahead for twelve minutes to the hill above **Greenway** to capture superb views of the **River Dart**.

So, going straight on, we bear right down a track to a lane and turn left, heading past the **Maypool YHA** to a field gate; entering National Trust land we continue along the top edge of the field to an information board (Wp.6

views downstream to Dartmouth

90M). From here along the *ria* there are excellent views downstream to **Dartmouth**; far below, between densely wooded slopes the gradually broadening river courses its way to the sea. Turning right through two gates, it's a short stroll along a field edge to the hilltop and a further splendid vista (Wp.7 94M/0M) where the **Dart** swings sharply around the white settlement of **Dittisham** as the incoming tide flows up to **Totnes**.

Greenway House

The original Greenway Court was constructed in the reign of Henry VIII for the Gilbert family of merchant adventurers; Sir Walter Raleigh, England's initial tobacco importer is reputed to have smoked his first pipe in the boat house. The current **Greenway House** built in 1791 sits in a stunning garden with magnificent views along the **River Dart**. It was bought by Agatha Christie and her husband in 1938 and used as a holiday home for 40 years before being gifted by the family to the National Trust in 2000. The estate is undergoing major restoration to further improve the garden and re-open the house and its many collections; the project is aimed at evoking the essence of a 1950's family holiday retreat.

To visit **Greenway** gardens and/or **Greenway Quay**, follow the signs and either catch the **Dartmouth** ferry or return to this point. Retracing our route past the YHA we turn right off the lane for 'Kingswear' (Wp.8 10M) to the path Y-junction at Wp.5. Now bearing right for 'Kingswear' we climb beside a field edge and go right over stile then left up a path past a manège, before swinging right through a gate into woodland. Gradually climbing a broad path into **Long Wood** we cross a stile (Wp.9 24M) and head right down a steep path before swinging left along the contour to a path junction. Turning sharp right, following the white on blue 'Dart Valley' trail signs, we descend steeply then swing left on a pleasant undulating path through open deciduous woods; emerging into an open landscape with views of the river, we can see

down to Noss Marina.

Dropping downhill into trees we head away from the river beside a creek; keeping right through a shallow ford (Wp.10 46M) we follow the track as it swings above a stream and climbs to a path junction (Wp.11 49M). Going right, a 'Dart Valley' marker directs us towards the main river before we bend gradually left to a lane; our route ahead continues through woodland, dropping down near the steam railway line before we climb steps to cross the A379 road. A 'Kingswear' sign points us ahead up a tarmac lane between houses, then we continue along concrete strips to a footpath signpost (Wp.12 64M); turning right our 'Pedestrian Route' descends between trees to a road, where we go left to a level crossing and the **Dartmouth** Higher Ferry slipway (Wp.13 68M). Turning left beside the railway our level path runs beside the estuary to **Kingswear**; time for a leisurely stroll, observing passing boats, noisy Oystercatchers and white Egrets paddling in the shallows. Going straight on past a level crossing we keep beside a coniferous hedge at the back of a marina then up a flight of steps onto a footbridge over the railway; a final climb to the road brings us to the banjo and the **Brixham** bus stop (Wp.14 84M).

beside the estuary to Kingswear

26 Kingswear, Froward Point & Scabbacombe Head

Kingswear from Dartmouth

Froward isn't misspelt, it means promontory, and there are points, headlands and promontories aplenty on this strenuous coastal walk from **Kingswear** to **Scabbacombe Head**; on the plus side, and it's a big plus, there is a terrific seascape, pine covered slopes and ever changing scenery. Our easier inland return along lanes and paths offers us inland vistas, sea glimpses and wonderful views from **Kingswear** across the yacht marina and through a forest of masts up the **Dart** estuary. En route, there's plenty of birdlife colonising the offshore islets, we visit a Coastwatch lookout point and there is a detour available to the National Trust house and gardens at **Coleton Fishacre**.

Shorter walks: there are several footpaths from **Froward Point** onwards that connect the coastpath to the return route e.g. between Wp.8 to Wp.13. 6.2 miles/ 10km A410m/D410m

Public transport: Stagecoach bus Nos. 22 & 24 from **Brixham**. Stagecoach bus No.120 from **Paignton**. The Torbay Steam railway operates seasonally from **Paignton**.
Access by car: Take A379 from **Torbay** to Hillhead then B3205 to **Kingswear**. Parking available in the Marina car park.

The Acorn marked coastpath starts just above the Lower Ferry slipway (Wp.1 0M) (SX 882510) where we go through an archway beside the Post Office, climb up Alma Steps and turn right along a lane that narrows to a tarmac path. In secluded gardens that surround us, the micro climate is warm enough to grow palms and other exotics; between the plants and roof tops there are glimpses to the estuary mouth and across to **Dartmouth Castle**. Going right along a lane (Wp.2 7M) through a dark canopy of laurels we bend right after Brookhill and climb to a Y-junction (Wp.3 17M); bearing left beside a house jauntily flying a skull and crossbones and a surprising knight in shining armour keeping a watchful eye, we curve left before leaving the lane at a coastpath sign. This next peaceful section through **Warren Woods** is dedicated to Lt Colonel H Jones VC, awarded a posthumous Victoria Cross during the Falklands conflict.

Turning right (Wp.4 20M) beneath trees down flights of sturdy wooden steps, we zigzag steeply into a valley and climb a stile onto a concrete track; going right then left, we trudge straight up a steep path into a wood. Briefly catching our breath, we immediately set off downhill but thankfully this time our pleasant path doesn't descend to sea level; instead we can enjoy beautiful views between tall Monterey pines to **Inner Froward Point** and back along the rocky shoreline into the **Dart**. Until a severe storm in 1990 this area was densely covered with 100 year old Corsican and Monterey pines; today National Trust rangers actively manage the area to conserve the landscape and ensure that hikers have good access. Our easier woodland path squeezes between a stile (Wp.5 39M), then after swinging around **Newfoundland Cove** and pausing at a well positioned bench, we wriggle between thorn bushes on our undulating way to **Inner Froward Point**. Inland, the imposing 80 foot stone tower has stood since 1864 as a navigational day beacon.

A signpost (Wp.6 50M) in front of concrete buildings that house the National Coastwatch observation point (see Box in Walk 28), offers a choice of routes for the next ¼ mile. The easier 5 minute cliff top route signed 'Brownstone car park' goes left for 200 yards then right on a 'Link to Coastpath, Brixham' along a grass track to a gate.

alternative concrete descent

The alternative concrete descent
Those wishing to faithfully follow the demanding twists and turns of the South West coastpath, are aficionados of WW11 memorabilia or have a passion for concrete, bear right for 'Brixham'. One advantage of descending the long flight of concrete steps between concrete batteries and bunkers is to admire the commanding view from the headland around much of **Start Bay**, the reason why the defensive gun emplacement was installed here. Staying beside a handrail for a short distance we bear left away from it and climb to an unsigned fork (Wp.7 58M); after keeping right between tree stump reminders of the 1990 storm, we make a long zigzag up to the cliff top path and bear right to a gate.

Now on open cliffs, our path uncoils down a hillside and with ever changing coastal views we switchback round **Outer Froward Point** above craggy bays

and coves before climbing to a path junction (Wp.8 83M); the 'Car Parks' pointer is a shortcut to Wp.13. Going straight on towards Puddicombe Cove sheltered by stands of pines, we drop down a woodland path to viewpoint benches at the entrance to **Coleton Fishacre**; this Arts and Crafts style house was built for the D'Oyly Cartes in 1925 - if the lovely valley gardens are open this is another shortcut that can be taken (entry fee for non National Trust members).

towards Puddicombe Cove

Climbing ahead for 'Sharkham Point' onto sloping cliffs, we arrive at a path junction (Wp.9 103M) above **Ivy Cove** and bear right for 'Scabbacombe Sands'; dropping towards a promontory we swing left down giant footprints and along to the next rocky inlet. Going round a valley mouth and traipsing uphill to cross a stile we bear left after a few paces on a level 'Link to Coleton Camp car park' (Wp.10 121M); staying high on the hillside above **Scabbacombe Head** there are grand views across to **Sharkham Point** and **Berry Head**.

the next rocky inlet

The *wustest* terrain is now behind us as we turn left beside a bench for 'Coleton Car Park' (Wp.11 126M), heading inland on a green path that widens into a track gradually ascending a broad ridge to a stile and signpost (Wp.12 142M). Bearing right for 'Brownstone' and

waypoint 12

strolling through a car park we arrive at a road junction; the fine house and gardens of **Coleton Fishacre** are down to our left. Our relaxing route goes straight on along a lane for 'Brownstone' towards a lonesome pine on the horizon; distant inland views roll across to **Dartmoor's** distinctive southern profile. After passing Coleton Farm (Wp.13 150M) and a car park, we descend to an inscribed **Brownstone** signpost (Wp.14 156M) and following 'Kingswear footpath' signs continue down beside holiday cottages; the lane becomes a track then dwindles to a narrow

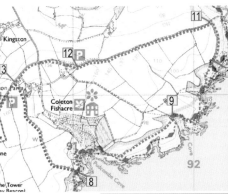

bedrock path dropping between high hedges into a valley. Taking care on the lower section which also contains a stream, we emerge beside a house and swing left along a lane; steep valley slopes topped with pine silhouettes lead the eye to the coast.

views over the Marina

Climbing a short distance, it's a pleasant return stroll to **Kingswear** along our outward route past the 'pirates' house and under the laurel canopy; at a Y-junction we fork left (Wp.15 184M) following a 'Coast Path' sign, then continue on a footpath past a black and white bollard. Wending between stone walls we go straight on past the top of Alma Steps, keeping left beside St Thomas's Church to Kingswear Hall and a T-junction (Wp.16 192M); with splendid views over the Marina we either turn left to the ferry slipway (193M) or right to the bus stop and car park (196M).

Dartmouth's coastal defences

Over the centuries **Dartmouth's** merchant and military ships have needed protection from seaward threat; **Dartmouth** and **Kingswear Castles** were built on either side of the estuary mouth both equipped with cannons and if required, connected with a defensive chain. Further upstream at **Bayard's Cove**, the narrowest point of the estuary, an artillery fort was constructed by **Dartmouth** Corporation in the early 16th century. During WW11 Brownstone Battery and observation post was sited at **Inner Froward Point**. Equipped with six inch guns and manned by 300 soldiers it protected the bay across to **Slapton Sands**; it even had a short miniature railway line to deliver shells to the guns. Today National Coastwatch volunteers man a lookout, providing an important observation service for mariners and others who use the sea and coastline.

This walk into picturesque nautical **Dartmouth** offers as much interest for walking legs as it does for sea legs with plenty of fascinating nooks and crannies to explore and idyllic spots to sit and wile away an hour or two. Steeped in maritime tradition this vibrant town in a wonderful setting is a delight to visit at any time of year and is best enjoyed at a leisurely stroll.

From **Little Dartmouth** on the western side of the estuary a coastal bridleway and permitted footpath brings us to splendid vistas on the heights of **Gallants Bower**. After a steep descent it's a pleasant promenade above the estuary into **Dartmouth** town and quayside; there's constant movement with changing tides and the toing and froing of yachts and ferries. Heading downstream to **Dartmouth Castle**, either on foot or by seasonal ferry, we climb the undulating coastpath enjoying lovely views of **Start Bay**.

2/3   2¼H   6.3 miles/10km   280m / 280m   4

Shorter walk: Omit the section into **Dartmouth** by turning right at the junction of Warfleet Road and Castle Road 4.6 miles/7.4 km A230m/D230m
Stroll: Turn right at Wp.2 to rejoin walk at Wp.13 1.3 miles/2.1km A/D 60m
Extension: Walk into **Dartmouth** and take the seasonal ferry to **Greenway** Quay to join 25 Shorter walk B to **Kingswear**. Catch the ferry back to **Dartmouth** and rejoin this walk at Wp.8 11¼ miles/18.1km A450m/D450m

Public transport: It's easier to start and finish at Wp.8 in **Dartmouth**. Buses include No.93 from **Plymouth** and No.111 from **Torquay**.
Access by car: From junction with A3122 take A379 from **Dartmouth** towards **Stoke Fleming** for 1½ miles; turn sharp left on B3205 then right at first crossroads. Park in the National Trust car park at **Little Dartmouth.**

Starting from the middle of the car park (Wp.1 0M) (SX874491) we take a 'Public Bridleway', strolling along a level hedge lined tarmac lane with coastal glimpses at field gates; going straight on between the farm buildings and houses forming **Little Dartmouth**, the 'Dartmouth Bridleway' now becomes an unmetalled track. At a stile on our right (Wp.2 7M), a footpath marker indicates a short cut to the coast path at Wp.13. Continuing along the track the views become grander, extending from **Start Point** over our right shoulder around **Start Bay** to **Froward Point**; here, the distinctive daymark beacon is used by ships masters as a navigation aid. Following a gently curving track around the top of a steeply sloping field we exit through a kissing gate behind a group of houses and start descending a small lane.

River Dart

An important check point for us is a bench on the right with wonderful views across the turquoise mouth of the **River Dart** to a pine covered rocky headland; <u>30 yards beyond the bench</u> we go left on an unsigned permitted path (Wp.3 20M), winding gradually up through woodland to a kissing gate. Just beyond, after emerging from the trees, a small marker post carved with crossed cutlasses stands at a path junction (Wp.4 24M). Forking left we climb between earth and stone mounds onto the top of **Gallants Bower** (Wp.5 26M); it's easy to see why this vantage point was chosen as a defensive position. Below, is a magnificent panorama of **Dartmouth** town, the harbour and estuary; we can also see how the twisting river entrance has provided sheltered moorings for ships throughout the centuries.

Gallant's Bower

This well preserved example of a defensive fortification was erected by **Dartmouth's** Royalist garrison during the English Civil War. It was one of a pair of earthworks constructed on the cliffs of the **Dart** designed to defend the town from Parliamentarian attack from the west and east; both, however, became totally redundant when General Fairfax cunningly bypassed them by capturing the town from the north in January 1646. This Scheduled Ancient Monument has been cleared by National Trust to reveal the full extent of the fortification, with five bastions linked by substantial earth ramparts.

Turning our back to the estuary, we walk down for 20 yards and with a large ash tree on our right go through a wide gap in the bank; turning immediately right, we take a grass path down into the trees to a kissing gate. Going straight on across an intersection through springtime bluebell woods, our path falls steeply down the hillside eventually zigzagging into a lesser gradient before dropping between clipped garden hedges to a lane (Wp.6 35M). We turn right along Warfleet Road to a junction where the shorter route bears right for **Dartmouth Castle**. Going ahead for **Dartmouth** we share the raised pavement with sightseers and amblers while enjoying glorious views to **Kingswear**. Above us, houses and cottages are randomly stacked on the steep slopes and we lose count of the number of balconies erected to take advantage of this idyllic waterside setting. On the skyline ahead sits the imposing

Britannia Royal Naval College, its red brick façade etched with white painted windows frames. A level stroll brings us to Bayard's Hill (Wp.7 48M), a narrow lane on our right where we descend to the quay and bear left along Lower Street past the distractions of gift shops, cafes and galleries to the quaintly named Boat Float (Wp.8 53M). On our left there is plenty of history to explore in the Butterwalk Museum while ahead, the beautifully kept Royal Avenue gardens are worth visiting. Our route turns right to the Station restaurant; this was the only UK railway station ever built where trains never arrived! There were insufficient funds to build a bridge across the Dart and the line from **Paignton** ends instead at **Kingswear**. Going right past colourful merchant's houses to the end of the quay, we bear right and left to arrive back at **Bayard's Cove**. Now we go straight on along quayside cobbles past a public barometer into the circular ruins of a fort; ducking under the second arch from the right, we climb a hidden flight of steps to the road (Wp.9 61M).

merchants houses

2nd arch
from the right

Turning left, nautical house names catch our eye as we saunter by Wreck House, Seagulls and Creekside before turning left into Castle Road (72M). At a Y-junction we go left on a tarmac path above the left hand lane; familiar Acorn coastpath symbols and yellow markers now guide us for the rest of our walk. At the end of the path going left and right along a narrow lane, we ignore the castle entrance sign, passing **St Petrock's Church** on our way to **Dartmouth Castle** and tearooms (Wp.10 82M); continuing on for 'Warren Point' up stone steps, we turn left for 'Little Dartmouth' and immediately fork left on a tarmac path above a picnic area. Now its slow going with lots of steps as our path runs around a cove then zigzags up into the trees to a lane; going left beside Compass Cottage and immediately forking left, the tarmac soon becomes a level well beaten earth path. Strolling through woodland and exiting beside a natural stone buttress we descend to a jagged shoreline at **Blackstone Point** and swing right along a low level section of path before crossing a bridge and climbing steps to a stile (Wp.11 106M).

Heading inland, it's a short climb part way up a valley to a marker post (Wp.12 111M); bearing left along a contour path we go out through a gate, stretching our legs beside field edges to a gate ahead (Wp.13 121M). Swinging left downhill past a pond, we aim for a gap in a wall on the headland; to our left beyond spiny cliff edges and precipices is the lovely setting of the entrance to the **Dart** estuary. Turning right, onto a broad grass sward dotted with benches we stroll straight on up a gentle rise to a bench at the far end tucked under gorse bushes (Wp.14 130M), then turn right and head inland. On our left, the low coastline of **Slapton Sands** sweeping out to **Start Point** was used by Allied Forces in 1944 to practice D-Day landings. After bearing right through a kissing gate, a well used path beside the hedge is our return route to the car park (Wp.15 140M).

The **South Hams** is known as one of the most idyllic areas in Devon - it's rightly popular, correspondingly expensive and well worth a visit! This walk explores some of its stunning coastline with fabulous views both near and distant, taking us first to the most southerly point in **Devon, Prawle Point**. The **South West Coastal Path** then leads us on to **Start Point** with its famous lighthouse and our seaside expedition is rounded off by a visit to the lost village of **Hallsands** followed by a ramble across lovely rolling countryside back to **East Prawle**.

5 | 4¾H | 12 miles/19km | 490m / 490m | 3

Access by car: Quite simply, as this area is criss-crossed by so many small but beautiful lanes, it's simplest just to follow the road signs from **Kingsbridge**! However, as a guide - leave **Kingsbridge** on the A379 east towards **Frogmore** and **Slapton**. After 3 miles at **Frogmore** turn right towards **South Pool** and, around the end of the creek, follow signs for **East Prawle** (approx 3 miles) and park by the village green.

Shortcut: 6 ½ miles 10 km 2 ¼ hours Follow the route to Wp.7. Continue straight on uphill meeting the main route at Wp.18 turning left.

We leave East Pawle village green (Wp.1 0M) on the road towards the sea and Prawle Point (S), already being treated to some lovely views and, after 5 minutes where the road bends sharply left (Wp.2 5M), we continue straight (W) on a wide grassy track. Coming to a T-junction through a metal gate (Wp.3 21M) we turn left between walls, following yellow waymarks towards the sea with the craggy mass of **Gammon Head** bang in front of us.

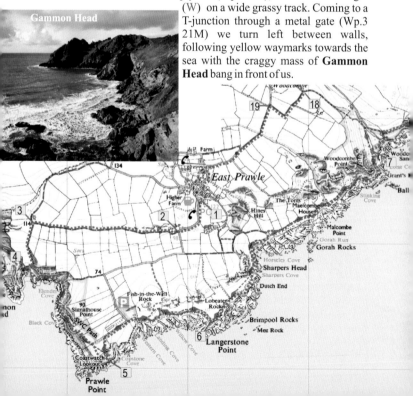

Gammon Head

The coastline is seriously dramatic here as we zigzag down to a junction with the **South West Coastal Path** with its familiar acorn waymarks (Wp.4 28M), where we turn left to follow it above a beautiful cove and beach east of the headland. This path, as coastal paths tend, takes us up and down a fair bit and we clamber round the rocky outcrops at the end of **Elender Cove**, the path being cut into the rocks above bringing us to the viewpoint above **Black Cove**. We're high up now with great views as we follow the path towards the **Coastwatch Lookout** at **Prawle Point** and, arriving there (Wp.5 48M) lose a few minutes admiring the volunteers and taking a peek at the visitor's centre; lots of interesting background information to be digested here (but no refreshments available).

Prawle Point

The flat lands of **Langerstone Point** now tempt us and, heading north at first on the path and ignoring a track from **East Prawle** coming in from the left, we make for the shore (Wp.6 65M) - at last an opportunity to explore some rocks and pools! Tearing ourselves away we set off round the point on a gentle climb in the general direction of the houses of **East Prawle** above on the left, the sea foaming on the rocks to our right. After 14 minutes, at the junction just past **Horseley Cove** we do a little dogleg to the left then right, always keeping to the coastal path towards **Lannacombe** and enter the grounds of handsome **Maelcombe House** through a gate - what a gorgeous spot! Leaving the house and grasslands for a narrow and sometimes slippery path uphill we pass through bracken and scrubby trees with rock pinnacles towering above making for **Woodcombe Point** - a great viewpoint. And, yes, if we go on round the corner for a minute there is a bench (thank you Frederick William Logan) just perfect for lunch and an admire of the birds playing on **Ballsaddle Rock** below. Some well-horned goats share this territory with us which can make it interesting but we set off again, refreshed, to a decision point at the next turning (Wp.7 100M). For the shortcut we continue straight on up and rejoin the main walk at Wp.18.

towards Lannacombe

For a really good tramp we follow the coastal path

right to **Woodcombe Sand** and then head down to petite **Lannacombe Beach** (Wp.8 113M), wild and beautiful, enjoyed by campers, caravanners and surfers quite apart from us. We climb again on a grassy track, keeping safely inland of the red markers warning of cliff erosion, fairly level easy walking now with a steep drop to the right and gorse clad craggy rocks on our left.

Two Stones

By the **Two Stones** (no surprises there) is another perfectly placed viewing seat from where we can contemplate whether we should conserve height or take a drop to **Great Mattiscombe Sand** - and then face the climb back up again! Whichever, we make our way to the far side of the beach and the crags of **Great Sleadon Rock** and rounding the headland we catch our first glimpse of **Start Point Lighthouse,** an impressive white structure, built to last.

With sheer drops to the sea below we watch our footing on the narrow path as we approach the spur and reaching the high point (Wp.9 161M) take time to absorb the magnificent views along the coastline both north along **Start Bay** and west where we have come from. A diversion to the lighthouse is warranted (Wp.10 168M), over the top to the access road and then right to the point but it's only open in the summer season.

Prawle and Start Points

These two Points and their accompanying sea-watch structures illustrate very neatly two organizations working for the benefit and safety of mariners. The first at **Prawle Point** is the National Coastwatch Institution which mans the lookout there. The lighthouse at **Start Point** comes under the auspices of Trinity House which is itself responsible for navigation aids for all mariners. The tall white circular tower with its distinctive parapet was established in 1836 and stands on the tip of one of the most exposed peninsulas on the English Coast. It's an essential guide to boats in the English Channel. The tower stands 28m tall, its cliff base taking it to 62m above sea level from where it has a 25 sea mile range of light, sounding for fog every 60 seconds.

Retracing our steps with great views across to **Beesands, Torcross** and **Slapton** beyond, we enter the carpark through a white gate (Wp.11 181M) and take the coast path to the lost village of **Hallsands**.

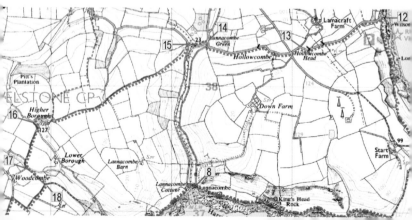

The tiny village of **Hallsands**, nestling between the cliffs and sea, was home to a small population of fishermen and their families in the eighteenth and nineteenth centuries; just 37 houses and a small chapel perching on the cliff and protected by a pebble beach. The 1890's saw the need for expansion of the naval dockyard at **Plymouth**, the building works requiring thousands of tons of

Hallsands

concrete and thus shingle was needed in vast quantities and conveniently there was plenty of this just nearby along the coast. Dredging began between **Hallsands** and **Beesands** and continued despite the concerns of the locals who feared for disturbance to their fishing livelihood and, as the beach was being lowered, a real threat to their homes from the sea. How right they were! Damage by autumn storms was obvious by 1900 and by 1902 six houses had disappeared and others required repairs. A new sea wall brought temporary respite to the village but on January 26th 1917 high tides and gales from the east combined together to breach the defences, just one house remaining habitable. The skeletal remains of the village can now be viewed from above but not visited!

The muddy/grassy path winds along and down bringing us to a cluster of houses, **Trouts** holiday complex, directly in front and the roofs of the ruined houses just visible below (Wp.12 196M). It's a good refreshment stop in summer and it's certainly worth following the track to the right to the viewing platform where the remains of the village can be seen clinging under the cliff. We turn left, inland, on the road at **Trouts** and then climb up to a T-junction (Wp.13 212M) where we turn left still on a narrow metalled lane, carrying straight on at the **Hollowcombe Head** crossing. Dropping into the pretty valley at **Lannacombe Green** we ignore a turning to the left coming to a cross-road (Wp.14 223M) bearing right, then turning left towards **South Allington**. Over a little stream we pass a ruined house, tropical palm trees highlighting the sheltered nature of the valley, then start to climb. As the road swings right we pick up a public bridleway to the left towards **East Prawle** (Wp.15 225M) and after negotiating the gate we turn immediately right steeply up the bank, the blue waymarked sign here is difficult to spot. The small track leads us gently up out of the trees and then, rather meanly, subjects us to a stiff climb to the top of the hill where, having caught our breath, we follow blue waymarks around a quick left then right. Field borders now guide us onward (SW) and we savour sea views left and a big vista right towards Dartmoor as we continue straight at a track junction towards **Higher Borough**. The signage directs us around the farm buildings on our left and, coming to a T-junction (Wp.16 252 M) we take the bridleway to the left for 50 yards and then turn right on a clearly signed broad stony access track. Level walking brings us to another diversion, this time around **Woodcombe**, and we turn left through a metal gate (Wp.17 257M) and aim for the gate opposite; the path here dips into a small valley and unfortunately a detour up to the right may be necessary in order to cross the boggy stream. Through the gate we join the shortcut route (Wp.18 264M) and turn right on a grassy path towards **East Prawle**, meeting a farm track and going right with it. With some relief as we near the village we turn left at the next T-junction (Wp.19 270M) and then, coming into the houses of **East Prawle**, turn left then left again past the **Pigs Nose** to regain our car (Wp.20 286M).

It's easy to understand why **Salcombe** is one of **Devon's** most popular resorts. It has everything: golden sands, a safe sheltered estuary surrounded by hidden creeks, a vibrant town and dramatic coastal walks. This walk explores the southern end of the estuary starting at **South Sands** and climbs past the lush, verdant gardens at **Overbecks** along the spectacular coast to **Bolt Head**. The secluded cove at **Soar Mill** tempts us for relaxation, paddling or rock pooling before our return to **Salcombe** along pretty Devon lanes and delightful wooded hills.

2/3   2½H   6.5 miles/10km   330m / 330m   4

Access by car: From **Salcombe** town follow the coast road south and park at **South Sands**. (N.B. There is an alternative parking at **Overbecks**).

We turn right (S) from the **Tides Reach** carpark (Wp.1 0M) at **South Sands** climbing gradually and keeping round to the left towards **Overbecks**. Passing between gateposts we continue straight into the **Overbecks** estate now managed by the National Trust and fork left off the access road onto the coastal path signed **Starehole** (Wp.2 6M).

Sharp Tor

As the track peters out we enter NT land signed 'Bolt Head' strolling through the trees high up on the cliff with great views of the sea below and **Limebury Point** opposite. This part of the estuary conceals the notorious **Salcombe Bar,** a narrow sea-covered spit of sand that restricts entrance to the estuary and has caused the wreck of many unfortunate vessels during bad weather. The path narrows and becomes more stony as we leave the trees making for the craggy rocks of **Sharp Tor** hanging overhead on the right taking a few moments to savour the view (Wp.3 16M).

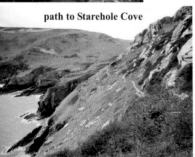

path to Starehole Cove

Setting off we climb steps cut in the rock through a cleft in the headland emerging on a vertiginous path precariously cut in the cliff face, a handrail on the left protecting us from the drop. Round **Sharp Tor** we head west dropping to **Starehole Cove** (Wp.4 26M) then swing left (S) starting the climb to **Bolt Head** on a steep path.

The tall jagged rocks of **Bolt Head** (Wp.5 36M) provide a prominent feature for seafarers navigating to the safety of **Salcombe** estuary. The views along the coast east and west are superb, gulls circle overhead warning us off, the occasional yacht or fishing boat passing by. The path continues with a short fairly steep section past a small gate then levels out as we stroll along with the steep cliffs on our left and a radio transmitter across the fields to our right. The transmitter originally a WWII radar transmitter is located at the site of the wartime **Bolt Head** airfield built as a satellite to **Exeter** and used by fighter aircraft escorting bombers to France. Ignoring a footpath right signed 'Marlborough' (Wp.6 60M) we carry straight on along a grassy path between low gorse to the north of **The Goat** headlands. An unusual conical building known as the **Signal House** (Wp.7 68M) stands to our right alongside a path to **Lower Soar** but we continue on the coastal path to **Soar Mill Cove.** High above the rocky **Steeple Cove** on our left we scan the rocks for the resting place of the **Cantabria** that ran aground in fog in December 1938 whose remains can reputedly still be seen at low tide. Past the next headland (Wp.8 73M) we start to descend steeply round a rocky outcrop seeing the **Ham Stone** clearly, a few yards off the coast, an island paradise for gannets and gulls, then clamber down into the tranquil, sandy **Soar Mill Cove** (Wp.9 88M).

Soar Mill Cove

If we can tear ourselves away from the beach we follow the path inland signed to **Higher Soar** climbing on a track across lush pasture up a shallow valley towards the low buildings of the **Soar Mill Cove Hotel**. Through a gate into the grounds of the hotel (Wp.10 96M) we keep left onto a small access lane and climb steadily past **Olde Cottage** at **Lower Soar** to a T-junction at **Higher Soar** (Wp.11 107M).

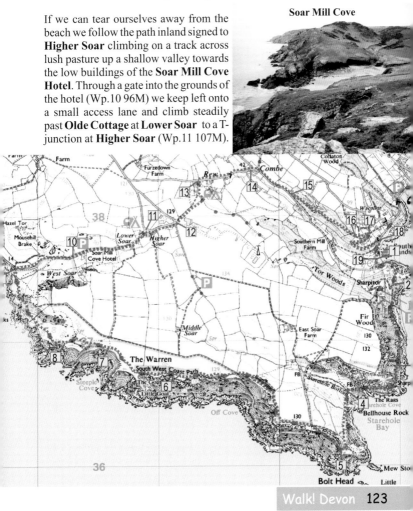

We turn right on the lane passing **Soar Farm** on the left and come to another T-junction after 250 yds (Wp.12 110M); here we carry straight on following a public footpath past some farm buildings then into a field alongside the hedge on our left. Dropping towards a cluster of houses below we keep the hedge on our left and join a track turning left through **Higher Rew Camping and Caravan Park** towards the site buildings and a road junction (Wp.13 117M). We turn right taking the narrow Devon lane through the hamlet of **Rew** down a steep hill to **Combe** where we cross over a stream and turn right at a road junction towards **Overbecks** (Wp.14 123M). Strolling past idyllic thatched cottages on the right between high banks studded with sweet smelling violets we come to **Briar Cottage** on the left (Wp.15 129M) and take a footpath forking obliquely left from the road climbing gently into the trees. The earthy path winds through the woods offering occasional glimpses of the **Salcombe** estuary ahead bringing us to houses high above **South Sands** (Wp.16 139M).

South Sands

We continue straight joining a residential road taking a sharp turn right at **de Courcy Road** (Wp.17 140M) to start zigzagging first on road, then path down towards the bay.

Joining the road at **South Sands** (Wp.18 146M) we turn right making our way alongside refreshment opportunities, gorgeous golden sands and sparkling seas back to our car (Wp.19 150M).

The coastline along the **South Hams** is particularly appealing for its contrasts: a secluded golden beach one moment, breathtaking views the next to say nothing of the dramatic cliffs with boiling seas below. This walk offers all of this and more! Our route takes us from **Thurlestone Sand** past the pretty settlements and coves at **Hope** to the magnificent viewpoint at **Bolt Tail**. From there we have a splendid coastal ramble to **Bolberry Down** followed by a gentle stroll across beautiful Devon countryside back to our start.

2 | 2¾H | 6.5 miles/10.5km | 270m / 270m | 3

Access by car: On the A381 **Kingsbridge** to **Salcombe** road after 3 miles take the right turn towards **South Huish**. Keep right in the village down to **Thurlestone Sand**.

We look out at **Thurlestone Rock** dominating this gorgeous sandy bay before we head south from the carpark (Wp.1 0M) on a lane towards the apartments perched on the cliff edge. A bird reserve with geese and the occasional heron and egret on our left distracts us as we stroll to a left bend in the road (Wp.2 4M) and turn right following the coastal path signs on a small access lane. After 150yds we leave the lane following the signs straight on through a wooden gate onto a gravel path leading to the cliff top with **Thurlestone Rock** on the right now revealing its hollow centre.

Thurlestone Rock

The path climbs gently following the cliff with the sea foaming on the rocks below and there's precious little protection from the steep drop. We ignore a path to **Galmpton** on the left (Wp.3 17M) continuing on the coastal path then dropping towards the houses at **Hope Cove** ahead. The **Hope and Anchor Inn** (Wp.4 21M) has a prime location just above the small sandy bay at **Outer Hope** from where we bear right following the road past the **Old Colonial House** on the left then down by the beach at **Inner Hope**.

Lifeboat station

Hope Cove

We come to an impressive lifeboat station (Wp.5 30M) built in 1877 overseeing the slipway down onto the beach and take a flight of steps ahead

Bolt Tail

leading to an earthy path climbing through trees along the side of the bay.

The trees give way (Wp.6 35M) to open well-grazed grassland and we climb more steeply to the **Bolt Tail** headland in front of us. The views from the promontory (Wp.7 43M) are breathtaking with vertical cliffs on three sides plunging into the water below, seagulls screaming and circling our heads. From **Bolt Tail** we continue with the coastal path (SE) past **Redrot Cove** and carry straight on at a stile (Wp.8 57M) above **Greystone Ledge** ignoring the path back to **Hope Cove** on the left.

The path undulates as it hugs the cliff edge and we pass through a gate (Wp.9 72M) at the top of a rise onto **Bolberry Down**, open grazing land enclosed by the upright stones of a *Bronze Age* boundary wall.

We see little evidence of the old WWII radar station that was sited here as we make our way turning right at a road junction near the **Port Light Restaurant and Inn** along to a car park (Wp.10 85M). Leaving the car park to go inland on a lane towards **Bolberry** past a radio mast, we drop gently first then steeply to a road junction (Wp.11 93M). Here we turn left signed 'Hope Cove' then almost immediately right down by red corrugated farm buildings. Crossing a

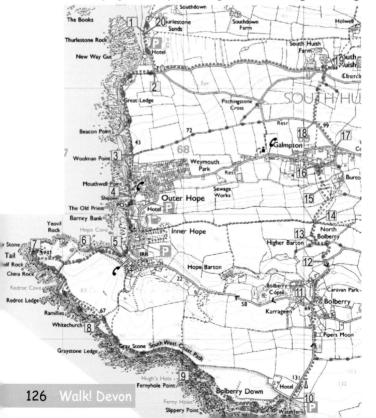

stream we wind our way between high
hedges past a thatched cottage and, as the
road bends right, (Wp.12 103M) we go
straight on a small grassy path,
Sweethearts Lane, to a junction with the
access track to **Higher Barton** (Wp.13
106M). We turn left through a gate
towards the house then after 100yds take
the footpath right up steps on a narrow
path signed **Hope Cove** and **Galmpton**.
Following the signs through two fields
we come to a cross tracks (Wp.14 112M)

Spring Lambs

and continue straight on a path (NE) down towards **Burton Farm** in the
valley below. We leave the path at the next gate keeping left along the edge of
the field down to an exit stile (Wp.15 119M) to a muddy farm track which we
cross then head down to a small wooden bridge and up to the houses of
Galmpton. Along an alley we join a cul-de-sac taking us to a road junction
(Wp.16 124M) and turn right then left at the **Burton** junction after 100yds. As
the road bends right we continue straight on up a lane to a T- junction (Wp.17
128M) where we turn left then immediately right signed 'South Huish'. Still
climbing gently we follow the lane until it bends left and levels (Wp.18
132M) and take a footpath right (N) down into the valley. We see **Thurlestone**
on the skyline ahead and the square tower of the 13C ruined **South Huish**
church down to our right. Joining the road at **South Huish Cross** (Wp.19
139M) we turn left on the quiet lane towards **Thurlestone Sand** with the
imposing rock dominating the bay and follow the road right back to the car
park (Wp.20 159M).

We make no excuse for including this walk. **Burgh Island** and **Bigbury-on-Sea** just can't be missed and there are some tremendous views on the way! We start at the pretty village of **Ringmore** and make for the **Avon** estuary which leads us down to the gorgeous beach at **Bigbury** and the ever fascinating **Burgh Island**. We track the coast up to **Ayrmer Cove** and from here we have two options - a short route back to our start or we can extend our expedition quite considerably for a fabulous coastal walk followed by the beautiful **Erme** estuary and a stroll across lovely Devon countryside back to **Ringmore**.

Access by car: From **Modbury** take the A379 in the direction of **Kingsbridge** turning right after 1 ½ miles on to the B3392 towards **Bigbury** then right again at **St Ann's Chapel** to **Ringmore**. In the village follow the road left at the **Church** then fork right on to a track to a National Trust signed car park.

Shortcut 1 Follow the main route to Wp.11 and turn right back to the car park. (1½ hours, 7.5km 4 ½ miles)
Shortcut 2 From the car park take the exit towards **Ayrmer Cove** (SW) down a small path to join the main route at Wp.11 and turn right (NW). (3 hours 12 km 7 ½ miles)

We leave the car park (Wp.1 0M), not towards the coast but back into the village of **Ringmore**, keeping left at the road and past the phone box. As the road bends left and just past a post-box in the wall we turn right (Wp.2 4M) down a metalled access track with occasional houses, continuing on by **End House** to a kissing gate. Here we pick up yellow waymarks which lead us down and up quite a steep little valley to a gate and the road at the top of the hill (Wp.3 16M). Crossing straight over we continue our roller-coaster down and up to a cross-tracks; **Bigbury-on-Sea** is to the right but we step out straight on a dirt track towards **Cockleridge** and the **Avon** estuary. Great views all round here and as we near the road we see **Burgh Island** over to the right. To avoid traffic we turn right in the field (Wp.4 31M) downhill towards **Burgh Island**, now picking up the acorn signage for the **South West Coast Path** which will accompany us for much of this walk. Hitting the road at an overflow car park (Wp.5 38M) we cross it onto a narrow grassy track and trace round **Sharpland Point** down towards the road and beach (Wp.6 44M). Depending on the tide we can either hike along the road to the main car park and café (Wp.7 49M) or take a stroll on those gorgeous golden sands below.. A diversion to **Burgh Island** is a real must, the sea tractor is fascinating and the 12th century **Pilchard Inn** is all too welcoming.

Burgh Island

Famous for its hotel and sea tractor and loved by all who visit for its beauty and tranquility, **Burgh Island** is something special. The hotel with its chequered history of dereliction and renovation was first built in 1895 by George Chirgwin, a music hall singer, and his wife Rose. Sold in 1927 to 'Uncle Archie' Nettlefold, the hotel then took shape as an exotic white art deco cruiser and became a retreat for a rich and prestigious clientele, including Noel Coward, Agatha Christie (who wrote two of her novels on the island), Edward & Wallis and Churchill. Cared for by a series of owners over the years it now offers luxury and splendour in a fabulous setting. The **Pilchard Inn**, dating from 1336 and deriving its name from the local, but now extinct, pilchard fishing industry is perhaps more accessible for all. It can be enjoyed by a short walk over the sands at low tide or a ride on the unusual sea tractor which is owned by the hotel but open to the public; trip timings are dependent on tide and weather.

Sea Tractor — Pilchard Inn — Burgh Island

However, tearing ourselves away from this beauty spot, we follow signs 'Coast Path - Challaborough' from the car park emerging to the road by a red phone box and then heading along the coast round the back of the flats. We cross through the **Warren Car Park** meeting the road (Wp.8 54M) and turn left for 100 yards, then by **Rathvendon** (Wp.9 56M) we maintain our direction straight ahead on a gravel track as the road swings up to the right. Dropping to the caravans at **Challaborough** we go left at the recycling bank towards **Ayrmer Cove** as the road bends right over a speed hump (Wp.10 63M). This is a beautiful section of coastline with glorious views which apparently even basking sharks come to enjoy in summer but more present dangers for us lie in the unfenced and eroding cliff edge beside us. A steady climb brings us to the cliff top above **Black Stone** from where we descend steeply to **Ayrmer Cove** - sand and rock-pools await us (Wp.11 81M). A right turn here provides a shortcut back to the car but for more of a challenge we continue with the coast path towards **Westcombe Beach** on a stiff climb with yet more unprotected cliffs. There's never a dull moment as the birds entertain us with their acrobatics and hang-gliding and on a clear day we can even pick out the upright pillar of **Eddystone Lighthouse** away to the southwest.

Eddystone Lighthouse

The **Eddystone Lighthouse** lies 13 miles south of **Plymouth** marking a dangerous reef known as **The Stone** and on a clear day can be easily seen from the South Hams coast. Five lighthouses have been built on the site dating back to 1698. The first was constructed of wood and was unique in the world to be built in such an exposed location. However it lasted only four months before being damaged by heavy weather. The second and third lights lasted 4 and 47 years respectively and were followed by the first stone construction which lasted successfully for 120 years until 1880 when its foundations started to subside. The base stump of this tower is part of the distinctive landmark to be seen today as it squats alongside the present lighthouse while its top half was re-erected on **Plymouth Hoe** as a monument to the builder.

Zigzagging down sharply we arrive at **Westcombe Beach** (Wp.12 94M) only to struggle upwards yet again in the direction of **Erme Mouth**, a very well positioned viewing bench just waiting for us at the top at **Hoist Point**. Happily our path rolls more gently up and down ahead and we step out enjoying the wonderful vista and the great sense of freedom that this countryside inspires. Past **Broad Cliff Copse** and through a couple of kissing gates the headland at **The Beacon** (Wp.13 128M) gives us a breathtaking panorama: extensive sea and coastal views with a backdrop of **Dartmoor** inland, the appetising **Meadowsfoot Beach** in the foreground. At **Fernycombe Point** we are reminded of coastal erosion and still following our acorns we exit National Trust land and come to **Muxham Point** (Wp.14 147M) to discover the beautiful **Erme** estuary - its trees leading down to golden sands with birds, dogs and dog-walkers making a vibrant scene.

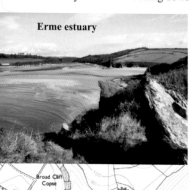

Erme estuary

As we continue on the coastal path into the river mouth it's possible to gain access to the sands at **Wonwell Beach** for a well-earned rest stop and then we're

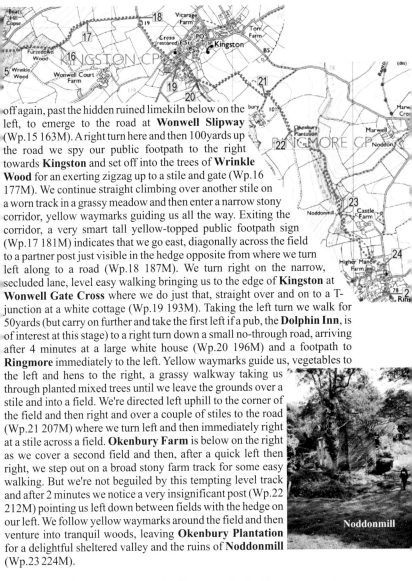

off again, past the hidden ruined limekiln below on the left, to emerge to the road at **Wonwell Slipway** (Wp.15 163M). A right turn here and then 100yards up the road we spy our public footpath to the right towards **Kingston** and set off into the trees of **Wrinkle Wood** for an exerting zigzag up to a stile and gate (Wp.16 177M). We continue straight climbing over another stile on a worn track in a grassy meadow and then enter a narrow stony corridor, yellow waymarks guiding us all the way. Exiting the corridor, a very smart tall yellow-topped public footpath sign (Wp.17 181M) indicates that we go east, diagonally across the field to a partner post just visible in the hedge opposite from where we turn left along to a road (Wp.18 187M). We turn right on the narrow, secluded lane, level easy walking bringing us to the edge of **Kingston** at **Wonwell Gate Cross** where we do just that, straight over and on to a T-junction at a white cottage (Wp.19 193M). Taking the left turn we walk for 50yards (but carry on further and take the first left if a pub, the **Dolphin Inn**, is of interest at this stage) to a right turn down a small no-through road, arriving after 4 minutes at a large white house (Wp.20 196M) and a footpath to **Ringmore** immediately to the left. Yellow waymarks guide us, vegetables to the left and hens to the right, a grassy walkway taking us through planted mixed trees until we leave the grounds over a stile and into a field. We're directed left uphill to the corner of the field and then right and over a couple of stiles to the road (Wp.21 207M) where we turn left and then immediately right at a stile across a field. **Okenbury Farm** is below on the right as we cover a second field and then, after a quick left then right, we step out on a broad stony farm track for some easy walking. But we're not beguiled by this tempting level track and after 2 minutes we notice a very insignificant post (Wp.22 212M) pointing us left down between fields with the hedge on our left. We follow yellow waymarks around the field and then venture into tranquil woods, leaving **Okenbury Plantation** for a delightful sheltered valley and the ruins of **Noddonmill** (Wp.23 224M).

Noddonmill

Forsaking the beautiful stream and valley we make for the trees up a stony track and, faced with a metal gate barring our way, settle for a mean climb to the right up a grassy hill. Passing **Castle Farm** with its turret on the left we negotiate a zigzag route with three kissing gates, always following the waymarks, until we come to the houses of **Ringmore** and a final somewhat tight kissing gate leading to a lane (Wp.24 236M). A right turn takes us to the junction by the church at **Ringmore Cross** where we turn right and, unless a diversion to the **Journey's End Inn** (200 yards to the right) is merited, follow the main road back to our car (Wp.25 245M).

The villages of **Noss Mayo** and **Newton Ferrers** overlook the **River Yealm** and whether visited by land or sea, are hidden from view until the last minute. The secluded estuary is a geological example of a *ria* and forms a stunning setting for the start and finish of this mainly coastal walk. For hundreds of years the twisting entrance protected working boats of fishermen and crabbers but nowadays it's predominantly the haunt of yachts and pleasure craft.

After a steady ascent on paths and fields we descend to **St Peters Church** at **Stoke Bay** then enjoy splendid scenery and relaxed walking along a 19th century coastal carriageway before turning into the wooded **Yealm** valley. This ideal year round route offers balmy summer strolls and invigorating winter exercise; after a south westerly buffeting it's always comforting to re-enter **Noss Mayo's** safe haven.

Note: walkers not wishing to tackle the steep drop from Wp.11 continue along the carriageway to Wp.13 avoiding the slight vertigo risk between Wps. 11 & 12.

3 | 2¾H | 7.9 miles/12.7km | 335m / 335m | 4

Public transport: First bus No.94 from **Plymouth**
Access by car: From **Plymouth** take A379 to **Yealmpton**, turning right on B3186 to **Newton Ferrers**; **Noss Mayo** village is on the far side of the creek follow upper lane past Church to car park beside tennis courts (SX 547474).

Shorter walk: From the car park turn left, climbing a lane signed 'Footpath to the Warren' for 15 minutes. At a T-junction, turn left, then right along a 'Footpath Link to Coast path' bearing right onto main walk at Wp.9. 4½ miles/7.2km A160m/D160m

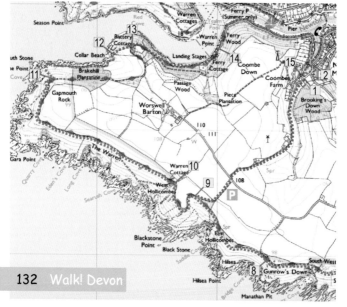

Leaving the car park (Wp.1 0M) and crossing into Foundry Lane, we bear right downhill between quaint cottages to the Village Hall (Wp.2 2M) and slipway at the head of **Voss Creek**. On entering Creekside Road we climb past the **Swan Inn** up Pillory Hill, with views to our left over **Newton Ferrers** and its squat church tower; many houses have picture windows and well positioned balconies taking advantage of the views and temperate climate. Going left down a

Voss Creek

lane at Junket Corner we continue as far as a large white cottage with a wavy roof, and turn right at a 'Public Footpath' signpost (Wp.3 13M).

Tarmac gives way to earth as we head up a yellow waymarked tree-lined path; climbing high above roof tops the gradient gradually eases as we pass between patches of naturalised clematis entwined through sharp thorn bushes. Over a stile we keep a shade left of the direction arrow, and as the field opens out in front of us, continue our gentle ascent towards a stile in the middle of the far left hand hedge. Surrounded by pastoral scenes and a backdrop of **Dartmoor's** southern slopes we cross into the next field bearing slightly right to another stile, then continue straight over a third field onto a lane (Wp.4 28M).

Turning left, a 5 minute stroll between hedgebanks brings us to **Stoke Cross**; going straight on down a winding lane past Revelstoke House, our first coastal views appear across **Bigbury Bay** to **Burgh Island** and **Bolt Tail**. Following a 'St Peters Church' sign (Wp.5 36M) we continue down a tarmac

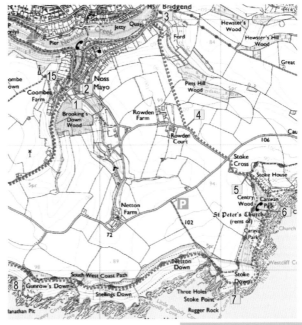

drive through the entrance to a well established caravan park tucked snugly between sloping cliffs. Natural jagged buttresses surround **Stoke Bay** and splinters of dark rock push out into the sea; in this isolated dramatic setting the consecrated ruins of **St Peters Church to the Poor Fishermen** are well worth visiting.

With the church on our left (Wp.6 41M) we head on under mature sweet chestnuts between carefully tended caravan plots enclosed by flowering hedges of escallonia and hydrangeas; keeping left at a Y-fork our track dwindles to a path wending through woodland before emerging onto a low open cliff. Following a grass path between gorse to a Y-junction (Wp.7 50M), a yellow arrow points us right as we climb uphill towards the **Revelstoke Drive** visible ahead as a faint line running just below the fields. Bearing left beside a stone pillar we are guided along this splendid carriageway by Acorn coastpath symbols; the timing from here to **Noss Mayo** is dependent on the weather and our inclination, either to stride out or saunter between various benches and vantage points.

Revelstoke Drive

The Lord of the Manor employed local fishermen during winter months to construct the carriageway so that he could show off his demesne to his guests. Leaving the now demolished Membland Hall after a late breakfast, their horse drawn carriages bowled through **Noss Mayo** and along the 9 mile drive.
Lunch would be taken at Warren Cottage and tea above **Stoke Bay,** far less exertion than our hike but very civilised!

Curving around **Snellings Down** there are fine views down the coast and ahead our sinuous route undulates along a flowing landscape to the far horizon.

rocky foreshores

Striking up a rhythm on the smooth grass and gravel surface with an accompanying sea symphony we enjoy expansive views of waves crashing into inlets and rocky foreshores. Rounding a walled bend on **Gunrow's Down** and passing a small building we keep left at a fork (Wp.8 76M) with views ahead of **Great Mew Stone** and **Plymouth Sound**; swinging round a broad valley and over a stile we climb to a junction with a gravel track (Wp.9 86M); here the shorter walk joins the coast path. Sweeping left then right round the headland we drop down to Warren Cottage passing through gates beside it (Wp.10 91M) and continue along a gently descending track; on a clear day **Eddystone Lighthouse** is visible on the horizon.

A mile further on above a square lookout our track swings right above **Wembury Bay** bringing welcome respite from prevailing winds. As our route again bends right above the estuary mouth we pass a stone wall with a bench to the seaward side then 100 yards beyond reach a bench on our right (Wp.11 111M). (See note in introduction). We turn sharp left on an unmarked path, dropping down a steep slope for 2 minutes; immediately above a white board, we bear right, gingerly finding our way down the grass to discover that the notice is a 6 knot speed limit sign. Unable to keep pace with the yachts we turn right, picking our way along a narrow uneven path, then climb a stile into Brakehill Plantation winding through trees and harts tongue ferns keeping roughly parallel with the cliff edge. Going through a kissing gate the path runs behind Cellars Beach to a T-junction (Wp.12 128M) where we turn left for 100 yards to explore this quiet sandy cove with its fine estuary views. Retracing our steps to the junction we go straight on, climbing a stony path cut between banks to Battery Cottage and turn left to rejoin **Revelstoke Drive** (Wp.13 132M).

Passing an Information Board immediately inside Passage Wood we continue for a few paces then bear left down a short flight of steps (135M); Acorn symbols and a yellow arrow point us along a pleasant oak wood path to Ferryman's Cottage. Resisting the temptation to pay 3d for 'Ferriage of Ass', we continue for 150 yards to a lane passing place; on our left is a signpost for **Kilpatrick Steps** (Wp.14 144M), a delightful contemplative waterside spot. Tearing ourselves away and ignoring the

River Yealm at
Kilpatrick Steps

Acorn coastpath sign, we bear right into an unmarked foliage tunnel on an undulating permissive path through Ferry Wood to the outskirts of **Noss Mayo**. Rejoining the lane, it's a short step to refreshments at the **Ship Inn**; just beyond, turning right at the village hall and climbing to the top of Foundry Lane (Wp.15 162M) we bear left to the car park (163M).

Starting a walk with a train ride is always a novelty and this excursion is no exception. After rattling along from **Bere Ferrers** to **Bere Alston** we hike down to the **River Tamar** and then enjoy a delightful stroll alongside the riverbank looking across to Cornwall. It's fascinating to observe the changing character of the river as it cuts through steeply wooded valleys to meander by reeds and mudflats, lazily making its way out to sea down a broad tidal estuary while we make our way back to our car.

Access by car:
From **Tavistock** take the A390 (initially towards **Plymouth** on the A386) turning left after 2 miles at the **Harvest Home** pub towards **Bere Alston**. At the **Rock** crossroads turn left on the B3257 still towards **Bere Alston** and after 3 miles (just before **Bere Alston**) turn left at **Quarry Cross** towards **Bere Ferrers**. In **Bere Ferrers** turn right into the main street, following the signs to the railway station and park.
Train times
About 7 trains a day run at approximately 2 hour intervals. For up-to-date details telephone National Rail Enquiries on 08457 484950.

Bere Ferrers Station

This lovely little Victorian station now doubles as a Heritage Centre with very unusual accommodation and a restaurant. Spend the night in a 1930's ex-LNER teak corridor carriage or dine in style in a refurbished restaurant car complete with liveried stewards! Or maybe just visit the collection of restored rolling stock, the handsome signal box and the quaint Booking Hall.
The station does however hide a darker side. A troop train halted here on 24 September 1917 - ten New Zealand soldiers stepped down to stretch their legs only to be struck by an oncoming express.

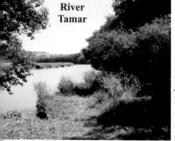

River Tamar

A pleasant five minute train journey from **Bere Ferrers** station brings us to **Bere Alston** (Wp.1 0M) where we alight and stroll through the small car park for 20 yards towards the road. Just before the junction we turn sharply back left (E) on a public bridleway waymarked with an apple, the **Tamar Valley Discovery Trail**, alongside the railway station and out towards houses and fields. At a small junction opposite **Fairmont** (Wp.24M) we swing left (N) on a public footpath into shady woodland, ignoring the signed path to the left over a ladder stile and take the small track to the right of a barred wooden gate.

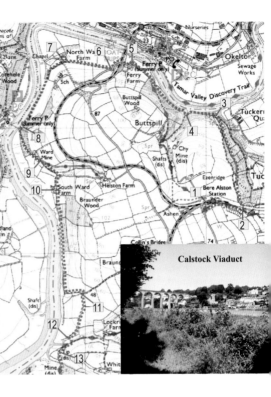

The pleasant secluded path leads us on downhill, the valley dropping away to our right, to water and white cottages (Wp.3 16M); the village of **Calstock** nestles dreamily on the hillside opposite, the **River Tamar** coursing lazily under the arches of the rail bridge.

Calstock Viaduct

We turn left (W) between a cottage and its river garden quickly heading back into woodland through a small gate for a gentle stroll alongside the water up to a broader track (Wp.4 20M). A diversion here to the right is tempting (if rather early) for a laze by the river so we follow the path of righteousness straight ahead across the track (NW) and up into trees on a narrow earthy track around the headland. Out in the open again our grassy way leads us towards the viaduct and **Ferry Farm** (Wp.5 29M); the footpath to the right is for the ferry but our stony path takes us left and up through the farmyard, with the likelihood of being ushered along by noisy but friendly dogs.

The track becomes a lane as we pass under the bridge, now heading uphill towards a signed public footpath (Wp.6 32M) and we turn right into a field (W) on a muddy track towards **North Ward Farm**. We cross the approach road and, wondering if we're actually trespassing into the garden of **North Ward Cottage** (we're not!), enter a narrow overgrown track through a rusty gate (Wp.7 38M) to the left of the cottage. A stile brings us out of the woods to a meadow with lovely views of the river and **Cotehele Quay** opposite then a two minute woodland stretch eventually brings us down to the water and a delicious resting spot by the jetty (Wp.8 48M).

opposite Cotehele Quay

Returning to our path we immediately bear left up into woodland on a broad track passing the 'ramblers' rest' picnic tables (a friendly touch) to **Ward Mine** and a fork right by some fenced dogs (not so friendly!) (Wp.9 54M). The slippery cattle grid leads to a gravel track and we're treated to gorgeous river views as we come down to **South Ward Farm** (Wp.10 59M). Keeping the farm on our right we make our way on the footpath alongside the river passing through a gate into scrubby woodland on a narrow earthy track. A wooden gate takes us into a rough field and 400yds on we turn left (E) and climb the grassy hill with woodland on our right; quite a steep little section this and almost at the top we turn right through a small metal gate (Wp.11 76M) to a little dip and emerge to another field. Ignoring the path to the left and following the hedge line ahead (S) we turn left at a tall yellow wooden marker post (Wp.12 83M) over a stile and into massive reeds - and it can be a bit boggy.

A two minute struggle across the creek and we are out to a right turn alongside the reed bed and then through a gate into a field (Wp.13 87M) where we bear slightly left on the trodden track across the field towards trees. Over a wooden footbridge and stile we negotiate a second creek to emerge through rough land to fields and follow the hedge line round and up to the left (S) with the river

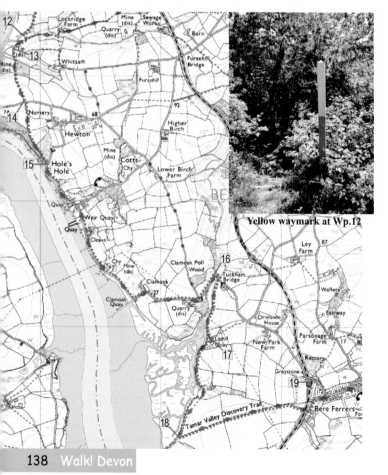

Yellow waymark at Wp.12

behind us. Arriving at a lane (Wp.14 99M) a quick left then right keeps us on the public footpath through grassy fields down to a stile into woodland, from where we are contained between fields to the road at **Hole's Hole** (Wp.15 108M). The river lures us to the right for a lovely waterside stroll along the lane with tempting resting places, the **Weir Quay** slipway near the boat club being our current favourite.

Weir Quay

We follow the road as it takes us up and away from the river (E) to a junction at **Tuckham Bridge** (Wp.16 133M) where it's possible to keep on directly back to **Bere Ferrers** but we prefer to turn right down the ladder-stile into a copse and out to fields. Keeping to the right and meeting pylons a couple of times we stroll down towards the river at **Liphill Quay** (Wp.17 146M) and are faced by another choice: if dry we venture towards the mud flats around the house to the right otherwise (and more probably) we follow the clearly posted signs to the left meeting the other path at the exit from the house.

Liphill Quay wet route

With the wetlands on our right and fields to the left the well managed **Tamar Valley Discovery Trail** leads us over walkways to a stile where we keep right along the edge of the field to a second stile (Wp.18 162M), tempting us towards the river. It's possible to scramble over and onwards here through the reeds to **Thorn Point** for some good views down the water to the **Tamar Bridge** but you'll have to retrace your steps! So from Wp.18 we turn acutely left (NE) up the grassy hillside, through a gate and under those pylons again to a rough vehicle track leading under the railway line. Past the houses our lane meets the road with the station clearly signed to the left and our car is just a couple of minutes away (Wp.19 182M).

This is a delightful and varied walk showcasing typical Devon countryside at its best. From **Buckland Monachorum** we get a taste of the gorgeous grounds of the **Garden House** before venturing over gentle pastures to the pretty village of **Milton Combe** with its quirky pub, the **Who'd Have Thought It**. **Buckland Abbey** (NT) then presents an opportunity for some interesting history before we make our way past **Denham Bridge** for a lovely river stroll returning cross-country to our start.

Access by car: From **Yelverton** on the A 386 **Plymouth** to **Tavistock** road turn west across **Roborough Down** through **Crapstone** to **Buckland Monachorum** and park near the church.

St Andrews Church

Setting off from the parking area in front of **St. Andrew's Church** (Wp.1 0M) we take the small path on the left between **Lady Modyford Hall** and the churchyard.

Turning right onto a footpath after 100yds we cross a small wooden bridge (Wp.2 4M) turning left alongside the stream in a grassy field. We climb steadily with the stream and trees on the left to a metal gate (Wp.3 8M) which takes us into the grounds of the **Garden House**, reputedly one of the most inspiring gardens in Britain occupying eight acres of land around the ruins of the medieval vicarage of **Buckland Monachorum**. Our path, lined with camellias and rhododendrons, skirts the attraction providing an occasional glimpse of the horticultural delights within then leads us right to the exit then into the carpark (Wp.4 15M). Turning right at the road we pass the driveway to **Crapstone House** and after 500yds turn left on a footpath climbing a few steps to a stile (Wp.5 21M) then striking out (SSE) across a grassy field. Waymarks lead us up into the next field with fine views on the right down to the **Tamar Bridge** then on to a junction (Wp.6 35M) where we maintain our direction and take the road signed 'Venton'. We stride out for 500yds and as the road bends sharply left we bear right through a gate (Wp.7 41M), struggle over a boggy patch then follow the public footpath down (SSW) to a gap in the hedge. Carrying straight on in the next field we cross a small meandering stream and turn left diagonally up to a kissing gate just below the buildings at **Broom** then continue to a road (Wp.8 55M). Straight across we pick up another footpath taking us alongside a hedge on the left across two more fields surrounded by the ever present patchwork of fields and woods on the rolling hills, to a gate and private driveway leading down to **Coombe Farm** (Wp.9 60M). Through the gate we are signed to go immediately right down steep steps into a valley crossing a small wooden footbridge then up to a road (Wp.10 62M) where we turn left past the grand farmhouse up to a T-junction. We turn right on the small lane climbing through trees then over a cattle grid on to **Clearbrook Common**. At the next road junction (Wp.11 75M) opposite **Covert House** we turn right then after 20yds left over a stile onto a muddy farm track alongside a low Devon bank with distant views of Dartmoor on the right. At a track T-junction (Wp.12 86M) we go right, downhill on a stony byway flanked by banks of primroses, violets and celandines heading for **Milton Combe**, following the track left at the next junction.

We leave the track at **Owls Barn** maintaining our direction through a metal gate (Wp.13 95M) onto a muddy path steeply downhill taking care on slippery steps cut in the stone, emerging by small cottages opposite the church in **Milton Combe** (Wp.14 99M). Turning right then immediately left past a telephone box and over a stream we reach the narrow main street running through the picturesque village facing a steep hillside, glorious with daffodils and primroses. Our way now take us right to a T-junction and the inviting **Who'd Have Thought It** 16C free house, reputedly named by the landlord in 1891 after his surprise at being granted a full licence.

Bearing left we're challenged with a stiff climb and cross directly over the main road at the top (Wp.15 105M) up steps to a stile and footpath. We pass to the rear of a bus lay-by then negotiate a kissing gate into a field to follow the

Who'd Have Thought It in Milton Combe

fence on the left and catch our first glimpses of **Buckland Abbey** through the trees. Over an access track we wander across closely cropped pasture arriving at the driveway into the **Abbey** (Wp.16 112M) with the square tower of the main building rising above the surrounding outbuildings on our left.

Buckland Abbey

Set in its own beautiful grounds and gardens **Buckland Abbey** has a rich and fascinating history. Home to Cistercian monks in the 13th century the monastery was sold by Henry VIII to Sir Richard Grenville who wished to provide an estate for his son, Roger. Due to the latter's death whilst commanding the 'Mary Rose' the property passed to his son, another Richard, who developed a fine home for his own use. Buckland was next to become one of the many domestic retreats of the famous sailor, Sir Francis Drake, afforded as a consequence of the rewards given to him by Queen Elizabeth I for his explorations and seafaring feats. The house has an unusual Tudor frieze in the splendid Great Hall and is known also for its magnificent monastic barn.

Continuing straight across the driveway (N) through a metal gate we follow the path across a verdant meadow down to a back road into the estate. Straight across the road and over a stream we climb up to the main road (Wp.17 115M) turning left and using the wide grass verges to avoid the traffic. After 500yds, at a road junction (Wp.18 122M) we turn left (straight on at this junction provides a quicker way back to **Buckland Monachorum**) dropping between trees into the **Tavy** valley and following the road alongside the river to beautiful **Denham Bridge** (Wp.19 138M).

Following the river, keeping it on our left we take the narrow lane up out of the valley between mossy banks then after **Denham Lodge** we bear left on a footpath (Wp.20 142M) back to the riverside on an access track. In the secluded wooded valley we pass a few cottages on the right and continue on a muddy path next to the fast flowing river through occasional patches of bamboo. Beyond a weir, a favourite playground for canoeists, the river changes its character becoming tranquil and smooth with a wide grassy bank - ideal for a picnic stop.

Onwards we reach the buildings of **Hatch Mill** (Wp.21 155M) and go straight through the grounds exiting right through a double metal gate to the lane. We climb steeply soon losing sight of the river in the deep cutting below coming to a T-junction after ½ mile (Wp.22 168M) and turning right towards **Buckland Monachorum**, its church tower across the valley on the right. Ignoring a turning left to **Coppicetown** we carry on uphill taking the path left up some steps and over a stile (Wp.23 177M) then heading across the field (W) towards the church. The footpath signs take us alongside a farm track to skirt the farmyard on our right, across a field full of old machinery and over a stile onto a residential road. We continue straight on meeting the main street in **Buckland Monachorum** opposite the **Drake Manor Inn** and turn left to rejoin our car outside the church (Wp.24 191M).

It's always calming to saunter beside tranquil waters and **Roadford Lake**, the South West's largest area of inland water, is the focal point of this walk offering lots of interest, big horizons and many surprising views. Our outward route via **Germansweek** is through a quiet flowing pastoral landscape, crisscrossed by hedges studded with copses and an excellent panorama to **Dartmoor's** northern fringe. After visiting **Roadford's** Information Centre and dam, our lakeside return along Culm grasslands passes a cob shelter and bird hide.

The walk is virtually a figure of eight, providing two shorter walks, one through **Germansweek** and the second, a level lakeside stroll.

Shorter walk A: Follow route to Wp.9, going straight on down lane to car park. 5.7 miles/9.2km A190m/D190m

Shorter walk B: Turn right up lane from car park, turning right to join walk at Wp.9. 4.9 miles/7.9km A100m/D100m

Access by car: **Roadford Lake** signed off the A30, 14 miles west of **Okehampton**. Follow **Roadford** signs for 1½ miles then turn right for 'Bratton Clovelly' and continue for 1 mile, passing **Gaddacombe Cross** to **Headson Crossroads**. Here, bear left signed **Germansweek** for ½ mile to **Headson** car park located in a dip on the left.

Turning left out of **Headson** car park (SX439916) (Wp.1 0M), its easy walking along a lane surrounded by pastures and glimpses of **Bodmin Moor** beyond the lake, a lovely backdrop to skeins of Canada geese winging their way into land. Going straight on at **Southweek Cross** we cross a bridge over an inlet; if the water level is low, trees stumps poke out of muddy shallows, part of the hedges that existed before the valley was flooded. Turning right at the far end of the bridge over a wooden ladder stile onto a 'Public Footpath' (Wp.2 26M), we stoop under low arching trees for 2 minutes then go left up a signed grass path swinging right through

to a high stile

a copse to a gate. Bearing diagonally right up a pasture to a high stile we duck under a holly bush and climb an overgrown fern covered rocky path, partly doubling up as a stream bed. Two Millennium yew trees stand near the gate of **St Germanus** and in the church porch is a reflective social comment 'once we had shops, school, post office and many farms, alas today our church stands alone maybe as much as it did 800 years ago'.

At a lane junction we turn right through **Germansweek**, going by some of the properties mentioned above and now converted to dwellings, past the Parish Hall and Rosemary and Tarragon cottages to Old Chapel and a signpost (Wp.3

47M); bearing right on a 'Public Footpath' the track becomes a grass covered cobbled surface dropping between high hedgebanks. Crossing a railway sleeper bridge we continue straight on downhill past a path junction (Wp.4 55M) to the valley floor; using a footbridge on our left over the **River Wolf** we start uphill to a path intersection (Wp.5 58M). Going straight on up a 'Public Footpath' our woodland track steadily ascends beside thick moss covered banks to a stile and into a field; the signpost is awry as our direction is slightly left up across the pasture through a gate and onto a lane.

With our main climbs now completed there are rolling pastoral scenes as we

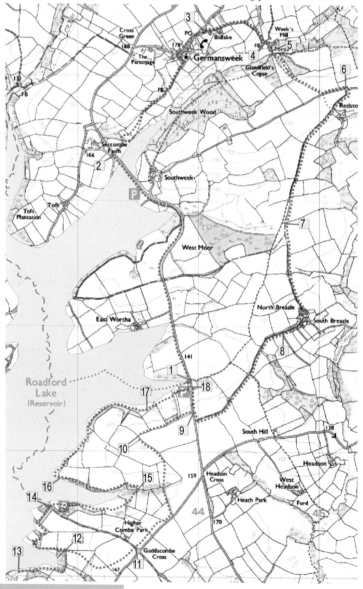

turn left a short way and then swing right onto a farm track 'Bridleway' (Wp.6 71M) going straight on beside the right hedge into a large field. Now striding out through pastures beside tree lined hedgerows it's a long gentle sweeping descent with fine views; in the far distance is the top of **Bodmin Moor** while to our left **Dartmoor's** northern skyline is reminiscent of ocean waves flowing south west to **Brentor's** *volcanic plug*. Walking beneath a long stand of mature oaks to a gate (Wp.7 86M), a blue marker points us slightly left across the next field to a protruding hedge corner and signpost. Going ahead

Dartmoor's northern skyline

beside the right hedge to a gate we join a muddy track to North and South Breazle, following signs into the farm yard and on through a blue signed metal pedestrian gate to a concrete lane. Turning right, a 'Bridlepath' sign points us into a grassy path (Wp.8 101M) before we bear left to rejoin the rough farm track; with glimpses of **Roadford Lake** we stretch our legs to a lane and turn right to a track junction (Wp.9 115M). **Headson** car park is 4 minutes down the lane.

Our route turns left (0M) on a level gravel track into **Roadford Forest**, part of a larger **South West Forest**; this ongoing project aims to significantly increase tree cover in an area bounded by **Bodmin Moor**, **Dartmoor** and **Exmoor**, helping bio-diversity, rural development and employment. Continuing beside a pleasant picnic area we go through a gate along a blue marked grass track past the first tree planted by South West Water; forking left at a junction (Wp.10 6M) on a 'cycle path' it's easy walking to the next junction where we bear left, still keeping on the 'cycle path'. Crossing a lane (Wp.11 20M), our gently winding trail, now signed 'Footpath to Dam', continues through blocks of conifers and mixed deciduous woodland, gradually curving right down to an enormous oak tree and a path junction (Wp.12 28M). Turning left we follow a gravel path above the lake to the visitors centre and café (Wp.13 35M), then suitably refreshed, return along the gravel path to the intersection at Wp.12.

Bearing left along a lakeside path past a shelter, we soon swing right onto a bluff graced by a circular grass topped cob shelter, traditionally built from clay, straw and other recycled local materials; a good vantage point for views of **Roadford's** dam wall and sinuous water line. Strolling on a gravel footpath beside coppices we cross a lane (Wp.14 50M) to a bird hide then swing right on a grass path, threading our way through clearings, trees and rough Culm

a cob shelter

grassland to a stile at the top of **Gaddacombe** inlet. Our homeward signs for 'Headson' start just inside a wood at a junction (Wp.15 61M) where we go left on a white circled path, swinging left along the far side of the inlet and out of the trees to arrive at a signpost that points right (Wp.16 71M). It's worthwhile,

the Headson path

however, going ahead a few paces to a promontory bench and wonderful lakeside panorama, before we complete the loop and regain the path, weaving between gorse, trees and grass clearings to a fork (Wp.17 86M). Going straight on for 'Headson' our final tramp along **South Wortha** inlet goes through a gate into trees and a lane (Wp.18 92M) where we turn left for 50 yards to the car park (93M).

Roadford Lake

Completed in 1990, covering 730 acres and holding 34,500 mega litres, Devon's largest reservoir supplies water for much of the county; a 430 metre long rockfill embankment constructed from local materials impounds water from the **River Wolf**. The Visitors Centre houses a fascinating exhibition depicting local history, the creation of the lake and how it is currently managed. Information Boards cover a variety of fauna and flora including two rarities, the marsh fritillary butterfly and Culm grasslands; this rough habitat of purple moorgrass and rush pastures was traditionally used for summer grazing of Devon Red beef cattle. There is a network of paths, cycle trails and easy access routes; the permissive walk to Headson may be closed during wet weather.

Sheepwash lies tucked away in a quiet rural corner of North West Devon. Once a self sufficient market town supporting over 50 trades it is now a sleepy village; it's large square complete with pump and bordered by thatched houses and the **Half Moon Inn** has a touch of rural France about it.

This relaxing walk through a gentle varied landscape along tracks, field and woodland paths is linked by short sections of lane; big sky's and wide vistas stretch far across the countryside to **Dartmoor**'s eastern tors. We pass the impressive **Buckland House** and can visit the adjoining church of **St Mary and Holy Trinity**. The route is well marked; yellow Devon markers, green 'Public Footpath' signs and red 'Ruby Country' waymarks - sometimes, all three at the same point!

Stroll: Turn left along lane after Wp.3 to Upcott Barton, turning left to rejoin walk at Wp.13 2½ miles/4km A95m/D95m

Shorter walk: Turn left along lane at Glebe Cottage Wp.7 rejoining walk at Wp.11. 5.9 miles/9.5km A150m/D150m

Access by car: From **Hatherleigh** or **Holsworthy** take A3072 to **Highampton**. **Sheepwash** lies 1½ miles north. Park in the village square (SS486063).

Leaving the village square (Wp.1 0M) on the **Petrockstowe** road between the pub and store we pass by cottages and North Road Farm before climbing a stile beside a 'Public Footpath' sign on our left (Wp.2 6M). Bearing right beside the hedge through three fields we go over a stile, descending the next field parallel to the right hedge some 40 yards away. Crossing a footbridge (Wp.3 17M) and climbing a pasture near the left hedge we go through a small metal gate and turn right along a track past farm buildings to a lane. Going straight across, the 'Public Footpath' is now a track up between fields; stony at first, it becomes a pleasant grassy surface as we stroll over a gentle crest, pausing to look back over broad pastoral views to eastern **Dartmoor**.

broad pastoral views

Dropping downhill and bearing left in front of Lake Farm a yellow way marker nailed to a telegraph pole points us round the house for a few yards; we turn left at an unsigned junction (Wp.4 30M), striding along a rough gravel track with a central grass strip. Passing a small group of houses at Buckland Mill we cross a stone bridge and bear right into coniferous woodland; going by a tall incongruous building, constructed mainly of railway sleepers, we wend our way along a level stone and earth track to a lane (Wp.5 47M).

Turning left up a short section of road, we exit the trees and just beyond a road

hipped lych gate

sign for **Buckland Filleigh** bear left into the driveway of **Buckland House** (Wp.6 55M) following a 'Public Footpath' sign. Turning left at the front corner of the house we swing right under a hipped lych gate beside the church of **St Mary and Holy Trinity** which has an unusual blue mosaic floor. With our back to the church door we go ahead down a path and over a stile; a stone faced ha-ha in front of the house and terrace gives uninterrupted parkland views and keeps livestock out. Keeping the lake on our left, we go

across a field and over a stream on a wooden footbridge; following red tipped footpath signs we climb diagonally right along the second forest ride from the right, to a lane (Wp.7 66M) in front of Glebe Cottage.

Going right over a stile through a fenced off paddock and over a second stile, we turn left along a field edge to a small direction marker post; striking across

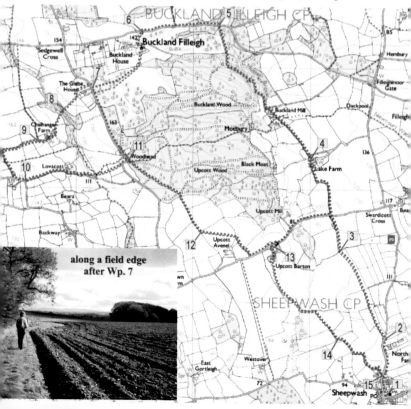

along a field edge
after Wp. 7

the field at right angles we descend to a woodland edge and down a steep flight of wooden steps (Wp.8 72M). After crossing a footbridge and stile we climb diagonally left up a field, then left along a rough track for 50 yards to a gate at Chalhanger Farm. Turning right we go between the buildings to a Y-junction (Wp.9 79M) and fork left on a level track to the far end of a field, then bend left to a lane.

Our route goes left for a short way before swinging left at a 'Public Footpath' sign down a track (Wp.10 88M); descending between bracken filled hedges we bear right beside Lovacott along a narrow pathway. After entering a wood we descend an attractive sunken track filled with ferns and gnarled tree trunks, cross a stream on railway sleepers and turn right through a gate. Our path continues over a footbridge and stile and keeping midway between the left hedge and the electricity poles it's a steep climb straight up through fields and over stiles to a lane. With **Dartmoor** views reappearing we keep left to Woodhead cottage (Wp.11 103M), then bear right through a kissing gate and after 20 yards swing right on a shaded 'Public Footpath' through the conifers. A wet and spongy earth track runs to the woodland edge where we turn right into a field alongside the left hedge; back into big skies and expansive views, we go halfway down the edge of a second field and turn left next to a broken down stile (Wp.12 115M).

Going diagonally right across a field in the direction of a flat roofed metal barn we aim for a 'Public Footpath' sign at the field corner and bear right down a track to a lane. Turning left along the road to a 'Footpath' sign we go right (Wp.13 123M) between farm buildings and through a gate on our right. Curving gently left down the length of a huge field beside the right hedge, **Sheepwash** gradually disappears into the folds of the landscape as we cross a stile heading for a footbridge in the trees. Crossing **Mussel Brook** and keeping left through a copse, we go over a stile into a field and climb beside the left bank to a tumble-down tree lined hedge that heads up to our right. Bearing right beside it to the crest, we continue ahead along a track to a gate (Wp.14 139M) displaying a 'Devon' footpath marker. Snaking up a *green lane* we stroll through two gates onto the village lane (Wp.15 146M) and bear right past a row of houses with neat enclosed porches to the village square (148M).

Buckland House

This imposing colonnaded mansion is a grade II Star listed building set in grounds of 289 acres. The land was given by William the Conqueror for services rendered, to Richard de Filleigh who had the original house built in the shape of an F. After a major fire the current residence was built in 1810 and having had a varied use

as a home, boarding school and adventure centre is currently a palatial 15 bedroom holiday home. So if you can get together a large enough party of walkers with delusions of grandeur and enough energy to dance till dawn in the two storey galleried ballroom, then this is just the place for you. www.bucklandhouse.co.uk

Hartland Quay is one of our favourite places whatever the season or weather. The magnificent natural setting is brought alive by powerful foaming seas crashing against rocks and sheer cliffs. Despite the fact that many ships have been wrecked on this notorious coastline, a working quay operated here for over two centuries; it was easier to bring supplies in by sea rather than land. Storm damage means that today little remains of the quay but the hotel, museum and Warren Beach are popular with visitors; for us the best time is a clear summers evening when an orangey red sun falls into the sea.

cliff formations at Warren Beach

Heading north up the coast, the terrain sets the scene for this exhilarating hike, plenty of ups and downs including steep flights of steps and wonderful vistas. The contorted geological cliff formations are fascinating; pressure of tectonic plate movements over millions of years has caused numerous bends, folds and waves in the rock strata. From **Hartland Point** we go inland, using ancient tracks and lanes past **Hartland Abbey** to **Stoke** and **St Nectans Church**. Continuing south to **Docton Mill**, we return to the cliffs and a spectacular waterfall at **Spekes Mill Mouth** and then enjoy fine sea views during our return **to Hartland Quay**. Between **Hartland Quay** and Point, several footpaths provide shortcuts to the inland section.

5 3½H 9.4 miles/15km 575m / 575m 3

Shorter walk A: At Wp.11 **St Nectans Church**, go straight on through churchyard and take footpath past coastguard cottages; turn right into field then left beside hedge along field edge to Wp.2 and return to start. 6.6 miles/10.6km A460m/D460m

Shorter walk B: Walk to Wp.2 then straight on past house and go into field on left. Follow footpath beside right hedge into **St Nectans** churchyard, exiting through lych gate and joining walk at Wp.11. 4 miles/6.4km A180m/A180m

Access by car: **Hartland Quay** is 15 miles west of **Bideford**. Take A39

descending towards the exposed coast (see next page)

towards **Bude** and turn right after 10 miles on B3248 into **Hartland**, and follow signs to **Stoke** and **Hartland Quay**. The car park is beside the hotel.

Starting at **Hartland Quay** car park (Wp.1 0M) (SS223247) we climb a lane to the first right hand bend; from here, familiar Acorn symbols and 'Coastpath' signs guide us to **Hartland Point**. Tackling a flight of steps, we pant our

way beside the cliff edge to a house at the hill top; turning left though a gate (Wp.2 8M) and heeding the yellow warning triangle, we set off along the left edge of a level pasture. After passing a ruined folly framing **Hartland Abbey** further up the valley, we descend towards the battered exposed coast; spiky rocks and storm beaches cannot prevent the grey slabbed cliffs from being eroded by powerful Atlantic storms.

Our path heads inland, delving into thorny scrub; going through a gate we turn left, descending over a footbridge and bearing left behind **Blackpool Mill** to a low cliff edge above a boulder strewn beach (Wp.3 25M). This is a good spot for a breather before a leg numbing ascent on a steep flight of steps, thankfully with splendid summit views then going right and left, we immediately descend across a field. Swinging left, our path crosses a stone bridge over the mouth of a rough valley before we climb the next switchback; now, with views back to **Hartland Quay** and ahead to **Hartland Point**, we head down parallel to the cliff edge before our rocky path bears slightly left plunging to a green valley floor. After strolling along a level path beside the high curving profile of Smoothlands we bear right

folded strata (next page)

out of the valley and along a field edge. Turning left, the coast path cuts down through dense bushes, over a footbridge and left to the cliff edge (Wp.4 59M); from this coastal *hanging valley*, dotted with sea thrift, a stream falls in short cascades to the beach. On our left the seaward side of Smoothlands is a sheer rock face and in front of it, folded strata give an impression of a gigantic ruined lime kiln.

Trudging uphill the gradient soon eases as we head along field edges with glimpses of **Hartland's** white topped lighthouse; in autumn an abundance of fungi is dwarfed by a giant white technological puffball on the far cliff top, an air traffic radar dome. At a 'Viewpoint' behind a lattice communications tower there are views of the Lighthouse. **Hartland Point** is Devon's most north westerly headland where the wild rugged Atlantic coast starts its southerly run towards Cornwall and was aptly called Hercules Promontory by the Romans.

Turning left (Wp.5 77M) down a concrete path to the car park and seasonal refreshment hut (Wp.6 81M) we head inland, bearing right along a tarmac lane past the unassuming Lundy Island Heliport and its ovine airfield maintenance crew then straight on down a blue marked 'Blegberry' bridleway. Going between farm buildings, much of our route to **Stoke** follows an ancient cobbled track connecting large isolated farms and hamlets. After a smooth raised grass section and a second gate, we go left (Wp.7 90M) at a 'Blegberry' sign, partly hidden in the right hand hedge, along the bank of a stream then cross a footbridge heading steadily uphill dwarfed by enormous hedgerows.

Swinging right at the brow, a short stretch of lane brings us to **Blegberry**, where we bear left (Wp.8 104M) into the next wide valley; there are broad pastoral views as our hedge lined path falls and rises to a lane at **Berry** (Wp.9 118M). Continuing ahead past a large renovated house and brick dovecote, the lane descends into woodland where stone built banks and iron railings enclose **Hartland Abbey's** deer park; originating from the 12th century, the Abbey was a monastery for 400 years and a family home since 1539. Climbing the lane past a 'Coast footpath' sign (Wp.10 129M) we head to **Stoke**, turning right up stone steps into **St Nectans** churchyard; the 39 metre tower, used as a maritime navigation aid, is the second highest in Devon and dominates the skyline during the rest of the walk.

Hartland Abbey

Leaving the south door we go left, exiting through an unusual lych gate (Wp.11 135M) (0M) with a pivoting central spindle, going ahead for 30 yards and turning right in front of Rose Cottage up an unsigned tarmac lane. Ascending to a broad hilltop we continue down a track into a small valley and after climbing past a farm, bear right along a lane. Heading south towards Cornwall the landscape and names assume a Cornish feel; strolling by Wargery and Trellick we descend to **Lymebridge** crossroads (Wp.12 29M).

The garden and tearoom at **Docton Mill** are 50 yards further on. Turning right for 'Milford' then right again onto a 'Public Footpath' we go along a valley track between trees and over a cattle grid; entering a wild valley we climb a hillock to a grass sward above **Speke's Mill Mouth**. It's a lovely place to quietly sit and marvel at the beautiful surroundings; to our left, **Milford Water** drops down rock slabs and pools to the beach some 50 metres below.

Going right (Wp.13 47M) up steps for 'Hartland' beside the cliff edge we promptly descend towards the rocky pinnacle of **St Catherine's Tor**, swinging right to go through a gate in a stone wall (Wp.14 56M) on a gently curving clear path behind the Tor. At the valley end, a large painted yellow arrow points us up the main track into a car park above **Hartland Quay** (Wp.15 65M) and final breathtaking views before we keep left down steps to the car park (67M); the pub is open all day for a welcome pint of Wrecker's Ale.

final breathtaking views

Tucked into the rugged North Devon Heritage coast, the Saxon settlement of **Bucks Mill** lies in a deep valley a few miles east of **Clovelly**. Fishing was once a mainstay of the local economy but when stocks fell, some inhabitants had to resort to a riskier occupation, sailing each day across rough seas to **Lundy Island** for work as quarrymen.

Climbing inland through woods and fields our pastoral route to the village of **Parkham** and the **Bell Inn** is along paths, a *green lane* and a quiet country road. Turning seaward to **Horns Cross** we follow a winding track, joining the coastpath above the red cliffs of secluded **Peppercombe Beach**; during a final energetic section along high wooded cliffs there are fine coastal views before a sharp descent to **Bucks Mill**.

3/4   3H   8 miles/12.9km   440m   440m   3

Access by bus: Nos 319, X18 and X19 between **Barnstaple**, **Bideford** and **Bude**. Get off at **Horns Cross** and start and finish walk at Wp.14.
Access by car: From **Bideford** take A39 towards **Clovelly**. After 8 miles turn right at **Bucks Cross** down a lane for ¾ mile to **Bucks Mill** car park.

Our start point is the village information board (Wp.1 0M) (SS 358233) located at the bottom corner of the car park. A short path brings us to a lane

and signpost indicating two footpaths; bearing half right (Wp.2 1M) over a gravelled surface and across a railed footbridge we squeeze between the houses, turning right behind a white cottage. Quickly leaving habitation behind our path ascends a wooded valley beside a stream on our right; after crossing a small footbridge the gradient increases as we swing right then gradually curve left out of the steep sided valley to a field. Striding beside the hedge to a stile we continue beside a barn

ascending a wooded valley

and between farm buildings to a path T-junction. Going right along a short grassy track and over a stile (Wp.3 18M) we turn immediately left, strolling beside the hedge through two level pastures to a curved metal kissing gate; far easier to negotiate with a back pack than traditional v-shaped types.

Going right to the busy A39 (Wp.4 24M) and carefully crossing onto an unsigned tarmac track we continue up a *green lane*, climbing between high hedgebanks to a crest; there are pastoral scenes at field gates with views back to **Bucks Mill** and ahead to **Parkham** church. Our track jinks right and left then descends into a small valley before climbing past a farm house to a lane (Wp.5 41M). Turning right uphill to a road triangle we bear left downhill for 'Bocombe', then go left through a field gate (Wp.6 44M) at a green 'Public footpath' sign, descending a path shaded by mature oaks into a small river meadow. Crossing a footbridge, we bear left along a steep grass slope to a stile

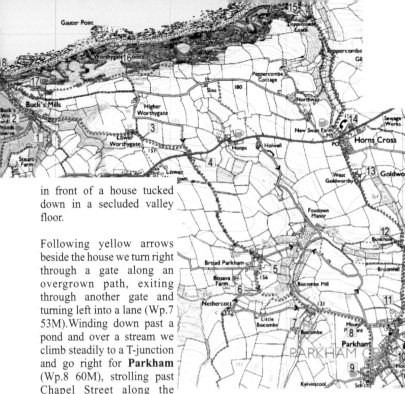

in front of a house tucked down in a secluded valley floor.

Following yellow arrows beside the house we turn right through a gate along an overgrown path, exiting through another gate and turning left into a lane (Wp.7 53M). Winding down past a pond and over a stream we climb steadily to a T-junction and go right for **Parkham** (Wp.8 60M), strolling past Chapel Street along the hilltop to a road junction; bearing right on the pavement, the welcoming **Bell Inn** awaits us serving good food and well kept ales. Dragging ourselves away, we turn left along Rectory Lane (Wp.9 66M) to a T-junction (Wp.10 70M) and go right to the church at **Parkham Green**. Continuing ahead, the lane bends sharp left, but we go straight on along a track past farm buildings, swinging left after 30 yards at a 'Public footpath' sign (Wp.11 75M) through a gate into a field.

Strolling downhill beside the left hedge and enjoying lovely valley views we go over a stile and straight on through a gate to a footbridge. Crossing a stream and going left up a track to the far end of a house, we bear right though an unsigned gate (Wp.12 84M); keeping beside a curving left hedge past a gate, we climb a stile and a flight of stone steps in a field corner. After negotiating a tricky stile, and keeping next to the fence for 100 yards, we bear diagonally left across a large field and with pleasant views behind continue to the top right corner and a stile hidden between broad hedgerows. The track leads through a farm yard where we fork left of a silage pit (Wp.13 94M) and join a concrete lane, gently ascending to a bungalow at the first bend; going ahead along the right field edge and over a stile, we walk down an earth ramp through a garage forecourt to **Horns Cross**.

lovely valley views

Turning right for 40 yards and re-crossing the A39 beside the **Coach and Horses Inn** (Wp.14 101M) we follow a **Peppercombe** sign down a narrow lane to a Y-junction and signpost. Time to toss a coin, as the waymarkings point in opposite directions to 'Peppercombe Valley, Coast path 1 mile'; both routes end up at the foot of the combe. Our choice is right into National Trust

Peppercombe Beach

land, steadily meandering down a stony track through deciduous woodland past a quaint thatched cottage before bearing right for 'Peppercombe Beach and Coast Path'. Our track wiggles its way beside a stream, past a ruined building and over a stone bridge to an Acorn marked sign pointing us sharp left for 'Bucks Mill' (Wp.15 117M); to visit **Peppercombe Beach**, a lovely secluded picnic spot, it's a ¼ mile return stroll.

lichen covered trees

an energetic stream

After a sharp stepped ascent we trudge up an earth path beneath moss covered trees to a field edge; our reward is a marvellous viewpoint around the sweep of **Barnstaple Bay**, a chromatic foreground of red and yellow cliffs melding into the dune fringed curve of **Saunton Sands**. Now on a defined cliff top path we can put the book away, following a clear coastpath to **Bucks Mill**; this roller coaster section includes several flights of steps. During a sylvan stroll we are enveloped in lichen covered trees, cool and peaceful in summer, but in winter bare branches allow clearer coastal views. At a path junction beside **Gauter Pool** (Wp.16 149M) we go straight on, starting the final mile to 'Bucks Mill' by climbing onto a ridge, then descending a narrow path beside fields through bracken and clumps of sloes. **Clovelly's** white cottages are tucked into the far cliff and flat topped **Lundy Island** sits on the horizon. Bearing right at a 'Bucks Mill' sign (Wp.17 162M) we descend through **Worthygate Wood** taking our time as the path becomes steeper and rockier before final twisting steps drop to a lane (Wp.18 170M); the Gut (slipway) and shingle beach are a few paces to the right. Turning left, we make our way up the lane beside an energetic stream, passing several pretty whitewashed cottages to the car park (176M).

This walk starts and ends with two superb stretches of coast path while sandwiched between is a quiet inland section along country paths and lanes. From **Croyde** village located on a deeply indented sandy bay, our route scales a belt of dunes then heads along the coast path to **Saunton Sands**. A steep climb gives a fine panorama over the lunar landscape of **Braunton Burrows** and north to **Woolacombe** and **Morte Point** before we head down secluded paths and byways to the coast; after a cliff top walk to **Baggy Point**, a final easy path descends beside a jagged shoreline to **Croyde Bay**.

There are two shorter routes for those wishing to linger on one or more of the fine sandy beaches.

Shorter walk A: Follow walk to Wp.11 and turn left along road to T-junction and right to car park. 4 miles/6.4km A165m/D165m

Shorter walk B: Turn right from car park and left along Jone's Hill to **The Manor** pub joining walk at Wp.11. 5.4 miles 8.7km A125m/D125m

Access by bus: No 308 from **Barnstaple**
Access by car: 10 miles from **Barnstaple**. Take A361 to **Braunton** and B3231 to **Croyde**. Car park behind Village Hall (SS 444392).

With our backs to the Village Hall (Wp.1 0M) we bear right along the street to the **Billy Budd Public House** (Wp.2 1M) and turn right on a 'Public Footpath to the Beach'. Strolling between walls and hedges to a gate (Wp.3 8M) set

Croyde Bay's sweeping beach

beside windswept evergreen trees, we go ahead over a grassy area, through another gate then straight on between ranch fences to a line of dunes. Swinging left and clambering slowly through soft sand, our view is around **Croyde Bay's** sweeping beach; after curving right round the rim of a large crater towards the sea, we descend gradually left, slipping and sliding down one of many small paths through marram grass onto the beach. Going left to the edge of the bay and along a rocky path beside a WWII bunker (Wp.4 19M), we cross a small beach and climb steps onto a low cliff and path junction (Wp.5 22M).

Turning right, our level 'Braunton Coast Path' winds between field edges and a shoreline of grey rock shards; in the bay behind us, dozens of tiny bobbing rubberised surfing ants wait for the perfect wave. Our path soon turns inland (Wp.6 30M) heading up steps past an old coastguard station to a road; going left for 100 yards we take care crossing over to regain the 'Coast path' (Wp.7 33M). Now it's easy relaxed walking to **Saunton** on a path running along a gorse packed hillside as we enjoy increasingly good views over **Barnstaple Bay** and kite surfers off **Saunton Beach**. Dropping to a path junction near the white exterior of the welcoming **Saunton Sands Hotel** we begin to appreciate the magnitude of **Braunton Burrows** sand spit and its landscape of hills and craters. At over 3,000 hectares, the UK's largest sand dune system is both a National Nature Reserve and UNESCO biosphere; stabilised by marram grass, there are over 500 species of flowering plants and a variety of beetles and butterflies. To visit **Saunton** beach turn right and follow the footpath down beside the hotel before re-climbing to this point.

Our route turns left (Wp.8 53M) on the 'Alternative coastpath', climbing steeply beside a small stream then swinging left up steps and over a stile into a field; from here the tees and greens of the links golf course sparkle like emeralds among enormous sand hills. Climbing to the ruins of a farm we bear left on a track signed 'Public Footpath to Croyde' (Wp.9 61M), swinging gradually right to the crest and through a pedestrian gate.

After going straight across hilltop fields to a double stile, we pause at Alf's seat to enjoy a lovely vista over **Croyde** and **Woolacombe Bays**. Camping is popular and in summer the valley floor is covered with a multitude of colourful tents; a contrast with the 1930's when beige and green canvas tents were the only choice. Going diagonally right down a narrow field path we climb stiles into a hidden

views after Wp. 9

path, plunging between hedgerows into the valley; after continuing through a kissing gate towards 'Croyde' (Wp.10 78M) we bear left onto a concrete drive for 25 yards, then fork right down an unsigned track between high banks to a lane. Just below is **The Manor Public House** (Wp.11 84M); shorter walk A goes left along the lane and Walk B joins the main walk here.

A 'Bridleway' sign to the right of the pub points us along a pavement that bends left to a 'Public Byway' sign; entering an earth track, we head up a valley wending between fields past Combas Farm, then along Meadow Lane to a gunnera edged pool at a T-junction (Wp.12 99M). Going left and taking care along a lane, we keep straight on at a junction to the crest above **Putsborough Beach** and a metal gate on our left set between concrete block pillars (Wp.13 104M). Climbing a stile onto the cliff we pick up 'Coast path' signs, and stay beside a wall for 200 yards to a signpost; bearing gradually right we aim for the right hand end of a tumbledown dry stone wall, going into a gorse lined path.

Entering National Trust land at a stile we revel in that marvellous combination of short springy turf and glorious coastal scenery, striding out on a well trodden path over stiles and skirting field edges. Bracken and gorse covered cliffs frame **Morte Bay** while endless surf rolls onto **Putsborough** and **Woolacombe Sands**. Arriving at a tall white post (Wp.14 138M) we go along a grass path a few steps to a Y-junction, forking right beside a fence protecting the cliff top, to a shaly path. Bearing right through a gate we zigzag down the headland and staying on the grey gravel path turn left (Wp.15 142M) above a huge inclined rock slab on which tiny white and yellow helmets of intrepid climbers may be seen.

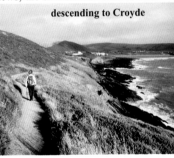
striding out

Our comfortable return to **Croyde** is an uplifting stretch of walking as we enjoy a gradual descent with wide sea views; the smooth headland in front looks like a sleek porpoise about to plunge into the waves and the low afternoon sun casts a terrific light, throwing long shadows across the bay onto a rocky foreshore. Going through a gate past a plaque commemorating Henry Williamson, the author of Tarka the Otter, our path becomes a track then a lane on the outskirts of **Croyde**. Bending inland (Wp.16 162M) along a path beside the lane, we turn right (Wp.17 166M) marked 'Public footpath' beside the surf school onto the beach. Here, going left across the sand we reach a stream and curve left in front of it into the dunes, crossing a footbridge and entering a path between ranch fencing to the junction with our outward route. Bearing left across a large open grass area to fir trees (Wp.18 178M), we return along the village path, turning left to the car park (186M).

descending to Croyde

Approaching **Mortehoe** the solid tower of **St Mary's** church stands proud of the skyline while the surrounding cottages, pubs and Heritage Centre are tucked into the lee of the hill, protected from Atlantic westerlies. This walk has a variety of landscapes, interesting historical connections and wonderful coastline vistas in an Area of Outstanding Natural Beauty.

Our outward route runs along short tracks and across fields past ancient farms, before dropping into **Borough Valley** and down a streamside path to **Lee**, a pretty setting with quaint buildings and masses of vivid summer fuchsias. In this secluded spot, crisscrossed with hidden paths, it's easy to envisage how wrecking and smuggling formed part of **Lee's** colourful history. A longer, more strenuous cliff return passes **Bull Lighthouse** and **Rockham Beach**, but rounding **Morte Point** the terrain gradually eases into **Woolacombe** and after a final climb to **Twitchen** we descend through fields to **Mortehoe**. There are several signed connecting paths from the Coastpath that provide short cuts back to **Mortehoe**.

4/5   4H   9.5 miles/15.3km   570m / 570m   4

Shorter walk: At Wp.2 turn left to **Rockham Beach** Wp.16 and left onto the main walk. 4½ miles A250m/D250m

Access by bus: No 32 from **Ilfracombe** and No 303 from **Barnstaple**
Access by car: **Mortehoe** is 13 miles NW from **Barnstaple**. Take A361 towards **Ilfracombe** and turn left at **Mullacott Cross** on B3343. Car park on left at edge of village (SS 458452).

With our back to the car park entrance (Wp.1 0M) we cross straight over into North Morte Road, signed Lighthouse and **Lee**, strolling between cottages past a footpath sign on our left to **Rockham Beach** (Wp.2 4M). Continuing to the end of the lane and a gate emblazoned **Bull Point Lighthouse** (Wp.3 7M)

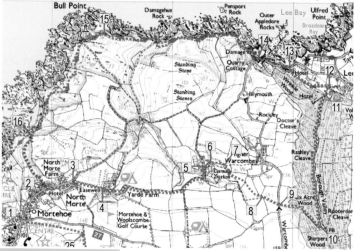

we turn right on a 'Footpath to Lee' into Easewell Farm camp site on a tarmac way; going straight on at a crossroads (Wp.4 10M) past the amenities block we descend a small path to the left of the clubhouse and out into countryside. Yellow markers point us between the buildings of Yarde Farm along a hedgerow lined grass path then up a man made gravel surface into a pasture.

Wp. 6

Keeping beside the left bank, with views of gorse covered slopes and glimpses of the **Bristol Channel**, we bear left onto a metalled lane, dropping past a pond and swinging right at the far end of Damage Barton Farmhouse. Going ahead (Wp.5 24M) for 'Walkham Farm and Borough Wood' we curve left to a footpath marker and turn right along a path for 50 yards. After going left through a yellow arrowed pedestrian gate (Wp.6 27M) we bear right, climbing through scrub land to a marker post displaying two yellow arrows (W7 29M). Here we keep right for 25 yards to a fingerpost and again keep right, initially along a track, before wending through large clumps of gorse guided to a field gate by small marker posts.

Bearing half right, we cross to a mound with a finger post perched on top and through a gate on our left (Wp.8 36M) into the next field. Ignoring a path ahead, we bear diagonally right over a hummock and a stile into a lane (Wp.9 39M); climbing into Access Land, we go straight across and over a stile into **Six Acre Wood**, dropping steeply down an earth path into **Borough Valley**. Turning left (Wp.10 47M) on a level 'Footpath for Lee' we wind beside a stream through ancient broadleaved woodland, filled with summer birdsong. After fifteen minutes, bearing right at a 'Public Footpath' sign (Wp.11 62M), we cross the stream and a stile, staying beside the right wall to a path T-junction (Wp.12 64M). We are standing in the sheltered **Lee Valley**, also known as fuchsia valley, its pretty cottage gardens full of summer blooms are enclosed with intricately patterned herringbone walls; the path to our right leads to the old **Grampus Inn**.

Our route goes left on a path between fields and down a lane to the bay (Wp.13 69M); stepping from country to coast, we turn left along a road beside rock pool heaven and climb steeply past the lovely Cliffe gardens to a 'Coast Path' sign on our right. Going right up steps (Wp.14 76M) onto Damage cliffs, Acorn Coastpath signs and symbols guide us on a fine hike through exhilarating scenery past **Bull Point Lighthouse** and **Morte Point** to **Woolacombe**. Inhaling delicately scented gorse we head off along the first stretch, 1¾ miles to **Bull Point Lighthouse**, with two sharp descents and ascents. Keeping left at a Y-fork, avoiding a steep flight of steeps, we descend to a footbridge and stile then zigzag up and over a cliff top and back to sea level; a second stiff climb brings us to an Acorn sign inscribed 'Bull Point' (Wp.15 114M) and the lighthouse just beyond.

looking over Lee Bay

Continuing behind the buildings and grey vertical slabs rising from the sea, we cross a green sward and climb a flight of steps before arriving above **Rockham Beach**; beyond the sandy cove we climb over a hill to a stile and signpost pointing left to **Morthoe** (Wp.16 141M). From here (0M) to **Morte Point** the terrain becomes less of a switchback, although our undulating path still twists and turns along sloping cliffs covered with drifts of springtime primroses; below, you may see bobbing grey seals and skimming oystercatchers. Sweeping views accompany us as we swing round **Morte Point** (Wp.17 29M) on a rocky path; treacherous currents and a reef between **Morte Point** and **Morte Stone** make this a notoriously dangerous area for shipping - in 1852, 5 ships foundered during winter storms.

Now striding towards **Woolacombe** our low level path passes **Windy Cove** and **Grunta beach** to a signpost for 'Mortehoe ¼ mile' (Wp.18 50M) just before the houses; we continue ahead through a gate in front of gardens following a path onto a road. Turning right downhill into **Woolacombe**, we bear right (WP.19 58M) across a grassy area above **Coombesgate beach** to rejoin the road and immediately cross over, going left (Wp.20 61M) onto a 'Public footpath. Climbing between houses to a field, we continue up the slope keeping right to a path T-junction (Wp.21 65M); turning left for 'Twitchen ¾ ' it's a steady climb along the Donkey Path, winding along the side of a valley between gorse and May blossom. Near the hilltop we climb a stile into light woodland and following yellows arrows keep to the right hand footpath past a pond up a short track to a T-junction (Wp.22 82M).

Turning left into the caravan park we bend right onto tarmac at a crest; looking diagonally left over the caravan site we can see a path beside a bank running uphill beyond the furthest caravans. To get there we go along the road for 80 yards to a green 'Public footpath' sign located just before gas tanks, and pointing left (Wp.23 85M) down a short path. A yellow arrow points us right into E field up a gravel track for 25 yards; as the track bends left (Wp.24 87M) we go right uphill between the caravans and turn immediately left between the first and second rows, walking for about 100 yards to a little post with a yellow arrow directing us right behind the next caravan to a stile. Finally clear of caravans, we stroll beside a bank made from thousands of narrow vertical stones up to a 'Morthoe' sign (Wp.25 92M); turning left over a stile we gently descend the length of a field to the village car park (97M).

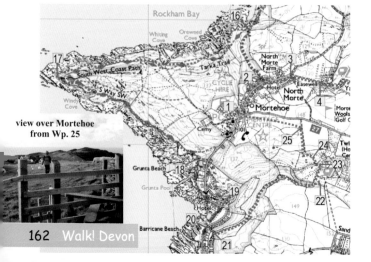

view over Mortehoe
from Wp. 25

WAYPOINT LISTS

See the notes on Using GPS around Devon on page 16; waypoints are quoted in OSGB datum BNG position format.

1
LYNTON, THE VALLEY OF ROCKS & WATERSMEET

Wp	Zo	East	North
1	SS	71904	49508
2	SS	71287	49823
3	SS	71020	49740
4	SS	71568	49214
5	SS	71715	49201
6	SS	71991	49262
7	SS	71990	48595
8	SS	72625	49016
9	SS	73999	48526
10	SS	74091	47751
11	SS	74396	48623
12	SS	74493	48854
13	SS	74259	49126
14	SS	74232	49508
15	SS	74049	49359
16	SS	73069	49533
17	SS	72276	49546
18	SS	72018	49489

2
DRY BRIDGE, SHILSTONE HILL & THE BRENDON VALLEY

Wp	Zo	East	North
1	SS	75949	45510
2	SS	75981	45924
3	SS	76120	46862
4	SS	75847	47212
5	SS	75819	47492
6	SS	75691	47708
7	SS	76307	47834
8	SS	76984	48223
9	SS	78070	47993
10	SS	78289	47877
11	SS	78361	47791
12	SS	78125	47366
13	SS	78076	46974
14	SS	78046	46514
15	SS	77708	45993
16	SS	76266	45342
17	SS	75973	45488

3
THE HEDDON VALLEY, PARRACOMBE & HIGHVEER POINT

Wp	Zo	East	North
1	SS	65521	48051
2	SS	65451	48188
3	SS	65453	47819
4	SS	65840	46734
5	SS	65590	45793
6	SS	66832	45023
7	SS	66831	44849
8	SS	67392	44936
9	SS	67119	45311
10	SS	67037	45813
11	SS	67628	46414
12	SS	66738	47135
13	SS	67387	47662
14	SS	67068	48577
15	SS	67372	48652
16	SS	66244	49426
17	SS	65520	48128

4
MOLLAND COMMON

Wp	Zo	East	North
1	SS	83496	29807
2	SS	83620	29966
3	SS	83235	30150
4	SS	82823	30550
5	SS	82991	31226
6	SS	81874	32134
7	SS	81570	32574
8	SS	81241	31848
9	SS	80489	30424
10	SS	79886	29200
11	SS	80242	28490
12	SS	80723	28362
13	SS	81194	28829
14	SS	81637	29216
15	SS	83183	29335
16	SS	83489	29789

5
AN EGGESFORD WOODLAND TRAIL

Wp	Zo	East	North
1	SS	69350	10541
2	SS	70016	10617
3	SS	70297	10417
4	SS	70203	09496
5	SS	69849	09056
6	SS	69654	08728
7	SS	69262	08706
8	SS	68558	07955
9	SS	67252	07746
10	SS	66719	07842
11	SS	66544	08373
12	SS	66554	08607
13	SS	66650	08841
14	SS	67869	09550
15	SS	67475	09673
16	SS	67815	10142
17	SS	67915	10534
18	SS	67654	10822
19	SS	68335	11245
20	SS	68883	11118

6
CHAWLEIGH & CHULMLEIGH

Wp	Zo	East	North
1	SS	71219	12627
2	SS	71700	12474
3	SS	72564	12224
4	SS	73573	12276
5	SS	73963	12229
6	SS	74119	12480
7	SS	73808	12910
8	SS	72420	13005
9	SS	72061	13131
10	SS	71982	13496
11	SS	71484	13931
12	SS	70523	13859
13	SS	70267	14342
14	SS	69908	14322
15	SS	68713	14247
16	SS	69078	13791
17	SS	69762	13807
18	SS	70577	13689
19	SS	70471	12818
20	SS	71189	12625

7
ZEAL MONACHORUM VILLAGE STROLL

Wp	Zo	East	North
1	SS	72078	03769
2	SS	71916	04019
3	SS	71749	04416
4	SS	71778	04675
5	SS	71302	04501
6	SS	70715	04453
7	SS	70805	04150
8	SS	71564	04301
9	SS	71822	04008
10	SS	72135	04143
11	SS	72373	04300
12	SS	72896	04526
13	SS	73170	04498
14	SS	72858	04307
15	SS	72647	03910
16	SS	72432	03547
17	SS	72340	03368
18	SS	71816	03269
19	SS	71986	03813

8

THE TIVERTON TRIANGLE

Wp	Zo	East	North
1	SS	95419	12497
2	SS	95144	12631
3	SS	94757	12736
4	SS	93260	12500
5	SS	92601	12667
6	SS	91642	12609
7	SS	90933	12611
8	SS	90981	12332
9	SS	90481	11892
10	SS	90924	11620
11	SS	91146	11297
12	SS	91439	11012
13	SS	91915	10435
14	SS	91707	10370
15	SS	91719	09576
16	SS	92163	09269
17	SS	92891	08385
18	SS	93208	07928
19	SS	93707	07609
20	SS	93885	07440
21	SS	95442	09704
22	SS	95478	10595
23	SS	95466	12104

9

A DASH INTO SOMERSET-WELLINGTON MONUMENT

Wp	Zo	East	North
1	ST	10249	13563
2	ST	10129	13988
3	ST	10219	14440
4	ST	10367	14539
5	ST	10508	14723
6	ST	10591	14827
7	ST	10808	15032
8	ST	10853	15117
9	ST	10907	14981
10	ST	11002	15082
11	ST	11173	15573
12	ST	11818	16473
13	ST	12005	16304
14	ST	12513	16668
15	ST	12813	16729
16	ST	13301	16863
17	ST	13797	17358
18	ST	13744	17257
19	ST	14332	16736
20	ST	13809	16769
21	ST	13822	15198
22	ST	13758	14972
23	ST	13431	14790
24	ST	13129	15308
24	ST	12935	15321
26	ST	12672	15275
27	ST	12440	15141
28	ST	12216	14953
29	ST	11826	14722
30	ST	11350	14675
31	ST	11077	14560
32	ST	11059	14391
33	ST	10957	14174
34	ST	10881	13956
35	ST	10903	13814
36	ST	10421	13595
37	ST	10258	13560

10

THE BLACKDOWN HILLS, KENTISBEARE & BROADHEMBURY

Wp	Zo	East	North
1	ST	09545	06857
2	ST	09755	08091
3	ST	09787	08669
4	ST	09443	09238
5	ST	09263	09392
6	ST	08871	09307
7	ST	08738	09295
8	ST	07066	09033
9	ST	06028	08816
10	ST	05750	08284
11	ST	06601	08188
12	ST	07161	07981
13	ST	07623	07391
14	ST	08046	06012
15	ST	09391	05340
16	ST	09992	04847
17	ST	10022	05192
18	ST	10197	06407
19	ST	09719	06912

11

STOCKLAND COUNTRY STROLL

Wp	Zo	East	North
1	ST	24854	04259
2	ST	25405	04431
3	ST	25678	04450
4	ST	25886	04019
5	ST	25906	03889
6	ST	25905	03736
7	ST	26296	03161
8	ST	26459	02696
9	ST	26437	02568
10	ST	26553	01490
11	ST	26177	01205
12	ST	25555	00876
13	ST	25374	01273
14	ST	25166	01387
15	ST	24996	01885
16	ST	25106	02292
17	ST	25105	02503
18	ST	24570	02858
19	ST	24249	03001
20	ST	23592	02697
21	ST	22838	03007
22	ST	22724	03421
23	ST	22972	03569
24	ST	23369	03577

12

SEATON TO COLYTON WITH A TRAM RIDE

Wp	Zo	East	North
1	SY	24681	90040
2	SY	24041	89824
3	SY	23885	89891
4	SY	23492	89665
5	SY	23378	89568
6	SY	22999	89191
7	SY	22837	89442
8	SY	22329	89566
9	SY	21056	89281
10	SY	21113	90503
11	SY	21122	91243
12	SY	21203	91383
13	SY	21028	91655
14	SY	20906	91737
15	SY	21138	92041
16	SY	21701	92618
17	SY	22107	92880
18	SY	21798	92327
19	SY	22579	92910
20	SY	22656	93483
21	SY	22911	93734
22	SY	23025	93853
23	SY	23492	94114
24	SY	23540	94304
25	SY	24485	94254
26	SY	24515	94143
27	SY	25170	94102

13

SEATON HOLE. BEER & BRANSCOMBE

Wp	Zo	East	North
1	SY	23491	89665
2	SY	23361	89556
3	SY	23144	89210
4	SY	23003	89192
5	SY	22862	88926
6	SY	22273	88042
7	SY	20961	88148
8	SY,	20691	88159
9	SY	20476	88212
10	SY	19209	88287
11	SY	18395	88278
12	SY	18423	88750
13	SY	18840	88855
14	SY	19724	88692
15	SY	19966	88640
16	SY	20743	88192
17	SY	21971	88149
18	SY	23041	89169

And a column from walk 12 (continued):

25	ST	23760	03854
26	ST	24466	04545
27	ST	24458	04642
28	ST	24827	04261

14
EAST HILL STRIPS FROM OTTERY ST MARY

Wp	Zo	East	North
1	SY	09428	95141
2	SY	09490	94899
3	SY	09558	94739
4	SY	09581	94522
5	SY	09691	94318
6	SY	10235	94225
7	SY	10463	94091
8	SY	10503	93888
9	SY	10709	93462
10	SY	11145	92668
11	SY	11351	92845
12	SY	11587	92437
13	SY	11228	91572
14	SY	11332	91124
15	SY	11158	90929
16	SY	11018	91025
17	SY	11000	90609
18	SY	10721	90088
19	SY	09160	91194
20	SY	09247	91743
21	SY	09196	91749
22	SY	09201	92384
23	SY	09387	94942
24	SY	09413	95148

15
OTTER ESTUARY AND JURASSIC COASTAL PATH

Wp	Zo	East	North
1	SY	07284	82115
2	SY	07482	83034
3	SY	07640	83017
4	SY	07773	81974
5	SY	09056	83666
6	SY	09221	83994
7	SY	09408	84702
8	SY	09660	85242
9	SY	10173	85712
10	SY	10346	85938
11	SY	10354	86200
12	SY	09451	85650
13	SY	08668	85288
14	SY	08405	85335
15	SY	07897	85273
16	SY	07753	84223
17	SY	07312	82134

16
EXPLORING WOODBURY CASTLE AND FIVE EAST DEVON COMMONS

Wp	Zo	East	North
1	SY	03247	87238
2	SY	03034	87304
3	SY	03002	86743
4	SY	03090	86518
5	SY	03174	86360
6	SY	03401	85702
7	SY	03678	85692
8	SY	03921	85546
9	SY	03718	85068
10	SY	03680	85042
11	SY	03691	84973
12	SY	03861	84848
13	SY	03815	84557
14	SY	03846	84469
15	SY	03796	84418
16	SY	03973	84226
17	SY	04046	83957
18	SY	04732	83498
19	SY	04888	83331
20	SY	05208	83465
21	SY	05252	83742
22	SY	05326	84042
23	SY	05415	84239
24	SY	05004	84338
25	SY	05149	85081
26	SY	05196	85648
27	SY	05364	85695
28	SY	05803	86447
29	SY	05621	86731
30	SY	05322	87302
31	SY	05709	87740
32	SY	05792	88515
33	SY	04711	88133
34	SY	04230	88013
35	SY	03334	87504
36	SY	03448	87353
37	SY	03340	87202
38	SY	03252	87247
39	SY	04018	84792
40	SY	04562	84494
41	SY	04746	84345
42	SY	04835	85938
43	SY	04836	86437
44	SY	04744	86690
45	SY	03651	87047

17
LUSTLEIGH, HENNOCK AND THE RESERVOIRS

Wp	Zo	East	North
1	SX	78507	81257
2	SX	78790	81201
3	SX	78873	81396
4	SX	78915	81387
5	SX	79178	80992
6	SX	79503	80774
7	SX	79892	81212
8	SX	79959	81310
9	SX	80553	80906
10	SX	80665	80815
11	SX	80753	80705
12	SX	80920	80872
13	SX	81624	79817
14	SX	81948	79744
15	SX	83046	80141
16	SX	83066	80866
17	SX	82904	81123
18	SX	82754	81403
19	SX	82049	81889
20	SX	81780	81857
21	SX	81372	82633
22	SX	81103	82692
23	SX	80439	82342
24	SX	80212	82416
25	SX	79935	82011
26	SX	79496	81737
27	SX	79263	81560
28	SX	79105	81552
29	SX	78509	81260

18
BLACKINGSTONE AND HELTOR ROCKS

Wp	Zo	East	North
1	SX	80296	88337
2	SX	80332	88294
3	SX	79949	87879
4	SX	79969	87610
5	SX	80115	87300
6	SX	80178	86669
7	SX	79996	86833
8	SX	79971	87035
9	SX	79792	86848
10	SX	78617	85747
11	SX	80049	85964
12	SX	80319	85782
13	SX	80610	85706
14	SX	80835	86024
15	SX	81243	85941
16	SX	81734	86536
17	SX	81846	87047
18	SX	81792	87408
19	SX	81691	87372
20	SX	81454	87445
21	SX	80799	87560
22	SX	80765	87785
23	SX	81114	88055
24	SX	80321	88293
25	SX	80306	88336

19

BELSTONE TO HANGINGSTONE HILL

Wp	Zo	East	North
1	SX	61986	93383
2	SX	61927	93556
3	SX	61619	93318
4	SX	61144	92884
5	SX	60715	92160
6	SX	60760	92063
7	SX	61025	91619
8	SX	61056	91505
9	SX	61116	90896
10	SX	61295	90025
11	SX	61384	89218
12	SX	61458	88589
13	SX	61316	87375
14	SX	61684	86187
15	SX	62222	87128
16	SX	62293	87715
17	SX	62041	88135
18	SX	61842	88697
19	SX	62094	89077
20	SX	62176	89308
21	SX	61975	91105
22	SX	61988	91420
23	SX	61751	91431
24	SX	62034	92964
25	SX	62002	93369

20

POSTBRIDGE AND BELLEVER TOR

Wp	Zo	East	North
1	SX	64673	78873
2	SX	64600	78676
3	SX	64544	78435
4	SX	64458	78218
5	SX	64398	77786
6	SX	64394	77662
7	SX	64495	77615
8	SX	64401	77497
9	SX	64465	77237
10	SX	64512	77124
11	SX	64476	76443
12	SX	64515	75844
13	SX	64940	75611
14	SX	65459	75539
15	SX	65573	75414
16	SX	65740	75585
17	SX	65803	75882
18	SX	66245	75744
19	SX	66415	75829
20	SX	66089	76456
21	SX	65987	76403
22	SX	65828	77339
23	SX	65636	77341
24	SX	65547	77424
25	SX	65121	77910
26	SX	64677	78855

21

STALL MOOR AND THE ERME VALLEY

Wp	Zo	East	North
1	SX	62546	61132
2	SX	62516	61598
3	SX	63218	62078
4	SX	63231	62527
5	SX	62989	63452
6	SX	62196	64860
7	SX	62500	65167
8	SX	63058	65596
9	SX	63622	65679
10	SX	63692	65506
11	SX	63607	65157
12	SX	63519	64456
13	SX	63551	64299
14	SX	63438	63807
15	SX	64012	63168
16	SX	63064	61213
17	SX	62807	61272
18	SX	62507	61111

22

EXPLORING HAYTOR FROM ILSINGTON

Wp	Zo	East	North
1	SX	78480	76154
2	SX	78369	76161
3	SX	77842	76499
4	SX	77655	77008
5	SX	77863	77338
6	SX	77044	77813
7	SX	76899	78080
8	SX	76608	78277
9	SX	76288	78972
10	SX	76226	78612
11	SX	76163	77755
12	SX	76091	77587
13	SX	76032	77462
14	SX	75864	77094
15	SX	75957	76744
16	SX	76147	76066
17	SX	76765	76089
18	SX	77129	75986
19	SX	77199	75785
20	SX	78205	74931
21	SX	78553	76093
22	SX	78562	76095

23

COASTAL PATH ST MARY CHURCH TO SHALDON

Wp	Zo	East	North
1	SX	92109	66122
2	SX	92423	66291
3	SX	92396	66567
4	SX	92590	67187
5	SX	92445	67312
6	SX	92437	67500
7	SX	92587	67625
8	SX	92695	67882
9	SX	92716	68180
10	SX	92720	68414
11	SX	92626	68512
12	SX	92856	69090
13	SX	93074	69616
14	SX	93051	69777
15	SX	93103	69986
16	SX	93219	70497
17	SX	93313	70912
18	SX	93425	71004
19	SX	93746	71629
20	SX	93814	71921

24

MARLDON TO TOTNES VIA TWO CASTLES

Wp	Zo	East	North
1	SX	86588	63203
2	SX	86502	63498
3	SX	86655	63601
4	SX	86815	64014
5	SX	86330	65614
6	SX	85487	65214
7	SX	85613	64555
8	SX	85434	63524
9	SX	84775	62831
10	SX	84218	62590
11	SX	84180	62499
12	SX	84111	62443
13	SX	83945	62311
14	SX	83665	62297
15	SX	82770	62317
16	SX	82566	62366
17	SX	82588	62502
18	SX	82209	62560
19	SX	82205	62201
20	SX	81024	60495
21	SX	80675	60013

25

BRIXHAM, GREENWAY & KINGSWEAR

Wp	Zo	East	North
1	SX	92579	56231
2	SX	91969	56873
3	SX	91853	56859
4	SX	90478	56306
5	SX	88144	54797
6	SX	87569	54676
7	SX	87502	54909
8	SX	88054	54836
9	SX	88118	54277
10	SX	88549	53349
11	SX	88657	53263
12	SX	88241	52458
13	SX	88206	52303
14	SX	88367	51150

26
KINGSWEAR, FROWARD POINT & SCABBACOMBE HEAD

Wp	Zo	East	North
1	SX	88186	51032
2	SX	88574	50886
3	SX	89063	50461
4	SX	89232	50464
5	SX	89886	49982
6	SX	90283	49704
7	SX	90310	49633
8	SX	91043	50414
9	SX	91825	50842
10	SX	92054	51042
11	SX	92159	51296
12	SX	92153	51583
13	SX	91041	51242
14	SX	90521	51130
15	SX	90206	50770
16	SX	88620	50867
17	SX	88221	51059

27
LITTLE DARTMOUTH & BIG DARTMOUTH

Wp	Zo	East	North
1	SX	87432	49134
2	SX	87941	49270
3	SX	88523	49877
4	SX	88400	50130
5	SX	88378	50180
6	SX	88046	50253
7	SX	87831	51018
8	SX	87820	51343
9	SX	87844	50965
10	SX	88664	50275
11	SX	88503	49429
12	SX	88386	49590
13	SX	88065	49024
14	SX	87914	48583
15	SX	87440	49086

28
EAST PRAWLE TO START POINT

Wp	Zo	East	North
1	SX	78103	36357
2	SX	77915	36097
3	SX	76721	36162
4	SX	76703	35814
5	SX	77331	35060
6	SX	78190	35401
7	SX	79519	36758
8	SX	80194	37214
9	SX	82463	37228
10	SX	82909	37162
11	SX	82098	37529
12	SX	81745	38547
13	SX	81069	38322
14	SX	80305	38351
15	SX	80136	38338
16	SX	78858	37718
17	SX	78795	37338
18	SX	78958	37220
19	SX	78683	37109
20	SX	78105	36350

29
A SALCOMBE STROLL TO BOLT HEAD AND SOAR MILL COVE

Wp	Zo	East	North
1	SX	72798	37651
2	SX	72967	37436
3	SX	72976	36794
4	SX	72553	36598
5	SX	72503	36136
6	SX	71165	36724
7	SX	70572	36952
8	SX	70222	36993
9	SX	69810	37589
10	SX	70296	37690
11	SX	70894	37891
12	SX	71149	37950
13	SX	71346	38284
14	SX	71780	38369
15	SX	72094	38183
16	SX	72631	37846
17	SX	72752	37856
18	SX	72857	37837
19	SX	72798	37651

30
BOLT TAIL FROM THURLESTONE ROCK

Wp	Zo	East	North
1	SX	67685	41445
2	SX	67765	41139
3	SX	67586	40449
4	SX	67574	40148
5	SX	67516	39678
6	SX	67269	39693
7	SX	66781	39650
8	SX	67341	39180
9	SX	68100	38799
10	SX	68889	38532
11	SX	69069	39274
12	SX	69175	39624
13	SX	69189	39767
14	SX	69085	39942
15	SX	69142	40208
16	SX	69120	40395
17	SX	69270	40534
18	SX	69083	40736
19	SX	69169	41144
20	SX	67690	41444

31
BIGBURY-ON-SEA TO RIVER ERME

Wp	Zo	East	North
1	SX	64993	45635
2	SX	65271	45849
3	SX	65643	45325
4	SX	66060	44661
5	SX	65643	44380
6	SX	65370	44259
7	SX	65090	44199
8	SX	64967	44454
9	SX	64994	44575
10	SX	64804	44970
11	SX	64156	45506
12	SX	63560	45827
13	SX	61748	46007
14	SX	61482	47006
15	SX	61994	47740
16	SX	62550	47863
17	SX	62799	48048
18	SX	63221	48079
19	SX	63542	47679
20	SX	63718	47560
21	SX	64279	47415
22	SX	64484	47134
23	SX	64889	46485
24	SX	65252	46077
25	SX	64996	45625

32
NOSS MAYO & THE REVELSTOKE DRIVE

Wp	Zo	East	North
1	SX	54719	47419
2	SX	54779	47545
3	SX	55430	47987
4	SX	55704	47146
5	SX	56206	46771
6	SX	56398	46466
7	SX	56149	45893
8	SX	54422	45976
9	SX	53855	46462
10	SX	53661	46552
11	SX	52683	47409
12	SX	53136	47608
13	SX	53292	47675
14	SX	54026	47674
15	SX	54704	47452

33
BERE ALSTON AND THE TAMAR VALLEY

Wp	Zo	East	North
1	SX	44022	67395
2	SX	44315	67353
3	SX	44102	68091
4	SX	43833	68101
5	SX	43399	68525
6	SX	43242	68474
7	SX	42832	68527

8	SX	42484	68025
9	SX	42643	67743
10	SX	42723	67511
11	SX	42959	66696
12	SX	42858	66340
13	SX	42782	66216
14	SX	42867	65799
15	SX	43057	65307
16	SX	44474	64425
17	SX	44422	63919
18	SX	44147	63127
19	SX	45247	63546

34

BUCKLAND MONACHORUM AND ABBEY

Wp	Zo	East	North
1	SX	48983	68352
2	SX	49128	68291
3	SX	49405	68251
4	SX	49658	68146
5	SX	49184	68098
6	SX	49632	67368
7	SX	49893	67090
8	SX	49929	66455
9	SX	50095	66188
10	SX	50079	66118
11	SX	50153	65457
12	SX	49400	65563
13	SX	48965	65917
14	SX	48848	65966
15	SX	48841	66329
16	SX	48920	66777
17	SX	48909	66991
18	SX	48806	67528
19	SX	47722	67830
20	SX	47731	68168
21	SX	46983	68194
22	SX	47553	68679
23	SX	48189	68440
24	SX	48982	68343

35

ROADFORD LAKE & GERMANSWEEK

Wp	Zo	East	North
1	SX	43938	91562
2	SX	43313	93357
3	SX	44041	94367
4	SX	44544	94284
5	SX	44604	94213
6	SX	45220	93908
7	SX	44709	92847
8	SX	44697	91961
9	SX	43950	91320
10	SX	43486	91124
11	SX	43475	90235
12	SX	42903	90218
13	SX	42508	90015
14	SX	42773	90558
15	SX	43486	90693

16	SX	42844	90787
17	SX	43586	91338
18	SX	43938	91509

36

SHEEPWASH & BUCKLAND FILLEIGH

Wp	Zo	East	North
1	SS	48649	06323
2	SS	48640	06787
3	SS	48266	07508
4	SS	48006	08258
5	SS	47212	09354
6	SS	46576	09306
7	SS	46133	08823
8	SS	45902	08657
9	SS	45675	08399
10	SS	45571	08059
11	SS	46434	08231
12	SS	47065	07653
13	SS	47657	07548
14	SS	48229	06793
15	SS	48624	06477

37

HERCULEAN EFFORTS AROUND HARTLAND

Wp	Zo	East	North
1	SS	22268	24719
2	SS	22623	24797
3	SS	22595	25710
4	SS	22905	26693
5	SS	23171	27570
6	SS	23510	27487
7	SS	23380	26843
8	SS	23263	26244
9	SS	23417	25454
10	SS	23710	24877
11	SS	23577	24687
12	SS	23641	22769
13	SS	22597	23605
14	SS	22637	24071
15	SS	22364	24686

38

BUCKS MILL, PARKHAM & PEPPERCOMBE

Wp	Zo	East	North
1	SS	35791	23255
2	SS	35793	23321
3	SS	36755	23140
4	SS	37145	22998
5	SS	37795	22141
6	SS	37770	21870
7	SS	38190	21721
8	SS	38684	21638
9	SS	38731	21162
10	SS	38843	21368
11	SS	39001	21714
12	SS	38962	22275
13	SS	38628	22727

14	SS	38472	23164
15	SS	38186	24145
16	SS	36622	23681
17	SS	35852	23477
18	SS	35520	23637

39

CROYDE, SAUNTON & BAGGY POINT

Wp	Zo	East	North
1	SS	44437	39216
2	SS	44450	39143
3	SS	43927	39175
4	SS	43480	38845
5	SS	43417	38752
6	SS	43171	38337
7	SS	43315	38404
8	SS	44782	37837
9	SS	44758	38002
10	SS	44725	38911
11	SS	44778	39210
12	SS	44814	40211
13	SS	44707	40431
14	SS	42198	40701
15	SS	42016	40595
16	SS	43308	39638
17	SS	43610	39586
18	SS	43930	39180

40

MORTHOE, LEE BAY & MORTE POINT

Wp	Zo	East	North
1	SS	45794	45243
2	SS	45956	45511
3	SS	46170	45570
4	SS	46420	45524
5	SS	47261	45675
6	SS	47330	45695
7	SS	47438	45688
8	SS	47746	45454
9	SS	47885	45396
10	SS	48240	45205
11	SS	48261	46262
12	SS	48297	46341
13	SS	47963	46487
14	SS	47689	46550
15	SS	46417	46728
16	SS	45823	45915
17	SS	44250	45542
18	SS	45440	44903
19	SS	45630	44508
20	SS	45500	44351
21	SS	45535	44276
22	SS	46411	44706
23	SS	46420	44833
24	SS	46362	44900
25	SS	46266	45150

Bound stone (Bond-stone, Boundary stone) - A boundary stone sometimes inscribed with the initials of a parish or landowner.

Bronze Age - A stage between the Stone and Iron Ages lasting in Britain from about 2500 BC to 500 BC when tools and weapons were made of bronze.

Cairn - A rough pile of stones built as a landmark, memorial or tomb.

Cist (or kistvaen) - A box-shaped burial chamber made from stone slabs.

Clitter - A scattered rockfield falling away from a tor.

Combe - A short valley or deep hollow

Froward - A promontory

Green Lanes - A network of historic tracks, some centuries old, providing links coast to coast and smugglers routes.

Hanging valley - Wave power erodes the coastline, leaving the upper part of a valley emerging from a cliff face

Hut circle - The circular remains of a simple stone dwelling with thatched roof.

Iron Age - The period following the Bronze Age, about 500 BC to 50 AD

Jurassic - Denoting the second period of the Mesozoic era lasting for 45 million years during which dinosaurs and ammonites flourished.

Leat - Manmade channel carrying water to power water wheel

Lynchets - Medieval cultivation strips caused by ploughing on a slope

Motte and bailey - Type of castle commonly built by the Normans, on a mound (motte) surrounded by an outer wall (bailey)

Overshot wheel - A vertical wheel turned by water which shoots over the top of it

Pound - An enclosure, usually circular. A simple pound could hold only animals. A larger pound could contain a whole prehistoric settlement with as many as 60 huts.

Ria - A drowned valley

Sessile oak woods - Native British oak with stalkless acorns: was often coppiced for timber and charcoal.

Stone Circle - A late Neolithic/Bronze Age free standing circle of stones possibly with ceremonial significance.

Stone Row - A late Neolithic/Bronze Age row of set stones often leading from a burial cairn or cist to a terminal stone (menhir). The longest known row in the world (4km) lies in the Erme valley on southern Dartmoor.

Tor - A prominent rock or heap of rocks.

Triassic - Denoting the first period of the Mesozoic era which began 225 million years ago

Volcanic plug - A mass of igneous rock filling a volcanic vent

Whetstone - Stone for sharpening instruments

Wustest - Worst of the worst (dialect)

Bibliography

Ancient Dartmoor – An Introduction, Paul White, Bossiney Books
ISBN 1-899383-22-0
A-Z of Devon Dialect, Chips Barber,Chips, Barber/Obelisk Publications
2000, ISBN 1-899073-96-5
Dark and Dastardly Dartmoor, Sally and Chips Barber, Obelisk
Publications, ISBN 0-946651-98-1
Dartmoor 365, John Hayward, Curlew Publications   ISBN 0-9514037-2-9
Dartmoor Stone, Stephen H. Woods, Devon Books ISBN 0-86114-843-6
The Devon Landscape, Devon County Council, Devon Books ISBN 1-85522-824-6
The Field Archaeology of Exmoor, Hazel Riley and Robert Wilson-North
(Exmoor Books) ISBN 1-873592-58-2
The Geology of Devon, Edited by E M Durrance & D J C Laming,
University of Exeter Press, ISBN 0-85989-247 6
The Hidden Places of Devon, David Gerrard, Travel Publishing Ltd, ISBN
1-902-00754-9
Medieval Dartmoor, Paul White, Bossiney Books   ISBN 1-899383-3-3
The Making of Modern Dartmoor, Bossiney Books   ISBN 1-899383-54-9
South West Coast Path Exmouth to Poole, Roland Tarr, Aurum Press
ISBN-10 1845132718
South West Coast Path Falmouth to Exmouth, Brian Le Messurier, Aurum
Press ISBN 1-85410-096-3
South West Coast Path Guide, South West Coast Path Association ISBN 0-907055-08-7 (updated annually)
South West Coast Path Minehead to Padstow, Roland Tarr, Aurum Press
ISBN 1-85410-415-2
Walk! Dartmoor, Kate & Alan Hobbs, Discovery Walking Guides ISBN 1-904946-12-7
Walk! Exmoor, David & Carol Hitt, Discovery Walking Guides ISBN 1-904946-18-6

Appendix A Websites/Useful Contact Information

Access Land www.countrysideaccess.gov.uk
Dartmoor Training Area (MOD) Tel 0800 458 4868 www.dartmoor-ranges.co.uk
Devon Tourist Information Line, PO Box 55, Barnstaple, EX32 8YR, Tel
0870 6085531
Discover Devon, Tel 0870 608 5531. www.discoverdevon.com
Exmoor: www.visit-exmoor.info
West Country Tourist Board Tel 01392 425426 www.westcountrynow.com
South West Coast Path Association Tel 017452 896237 - www.swcp.org.uk
General information www.information-britain.co.uk/tic

Tourist Information Centres

Ashburton, The Town Hall, Tel 01364 653426
Barnstaple The Square Tel 0845 4582003

Braunton Caen Car Park, Caen St Tel 01271 816400
Combe Martin Seacot, 13 Cross St Tel 01271 883319
Dartmouth, The Engine House, Mayor's Avenue, Tel 01803 834224
Exeter, Civic Centre, Tel 01392 265700
Okehampton, 3 West Street, Tel 01837 53020
Ilfracombe, The Landmark Tel 01271 863001
Kingsbridge, The Quay, Tel 01548 853195
Lynton Town Hall, Lynton Tel 01598 752225
Plymouth, Plymouth Mayflower, 3-5 The Barbican, Tel 01752 304849
Salcombe, Market Street, Tel 01548 843 927
South Molton 1 East St   Tel 01769 574122
Tiverton Phoenix Lane   Tel 01884 255827
Torquay, Vaughan Parade, Tel 0906 6801268
Totnes, Town Mill, Tel 01803 863168
Woolacombe The Esplanade Tel 01271 870554 (seasonal)

Appendix B Places of Interest

Dartmoor National Park Authority
Parke, Haytor Road, Bovey Tracey, Newton Abbott, Devon TQ13 9JQ
Tel 01626 832093 www.dartmoor-npa.gov.uk
DNPA Information Centres
Haytor Tel 01364 661520
Newbridge Tel 01364 631303
Postbridge Tel 01822 880272
Princetown (The High Moorland Visitor Centre) Tel 01822 890414

Exmoor National Park Administrative Offices
Exmoor House, Dulverton, Somerset, TA22 9HL
Tel 01398 323665 Fax 01398 323150 www.exmoor-nationalpark.gov.uk
Exmoor National Park Authority - Visitor Centres
Combe Martin - Seacot Cross St Tel/Fax 01271 883319 (seasonal)
Lynmouth – Lyndale Car Park Tel 01598 763466

National Trust in Devon www.nationaltrust.org.uk

Appendix C Local buses www.traveline.org.uk

Bus No	Route	Links with Walk Nos
309, 310	Barnstaple to Lynton	1, 3
300	Ilfracombe to Minehead	1,3
55	Exeter to Tiverton	8
20	Taunton to Seaton	9,12
X54	Exeter to Colyton	12
885	Axminster to Colyton	12
899	Sidmouth to Seaton	13
60,60A	Exeter to Ottery St Mary	14
382	Sidmouth to Feniton	14
387	Sidmouth to Taunton	14
380	Exeter to Axminster	14
157	Exeter to Sidmouth	15
357, 58	Exeter to Budleigh Salterton	15

56	Exeter to Exmouth	16
178	Newton Abbot to Moretonhampstead	17
82	Transmoor Link (Plymouth to Exeter)	18, 20
98	Tavistock to Yelverton	20
85	Exeter to Torquay	23
111	Torquay to Dartmouth	24, 27
12	Newton Abbot to Brixham	25
22,24	Brixham to Kingswear	25, 26
120	Paignton to Kingswear	25, 26
93	Plymouth to Dartmouth	27
606	Kingsbridge to Salcombe	29
162	Hope to Loddiswell	30
94	Plymouth to Noss Mayo	32
87	Tavistock to Bere Ferrers	33
55	Milton Combe to Yelverton	34
X18, X19 & 319	Barnstaple Bideford & Bude	38
308	Barnstaple to Georgeham	39
32	Ilfracombe to Mortehoe	40
303	Barnstaple to Woolacombe	40

Appendix D Devon's Long Distance Trails

Dart Valley Trail: 17 miles, Dartmouth, Totnes, Greenway, Kingswear
Dartmoor Way: 90 miles, Tavistock, Okehampton, Moretonhampstead,
                 Buckfastleigh, Tavistock
Devon Heartland Way: 45 miles, Okehampton to Stoke Canon
East Devon Way: 38 miles, Exmouth to Uplyme
Exe Valley Way: 45 miles, Exe Estuary to Exmoor
John Musgrave Heritage Trail: 35 miles Maidencombe to Brixham
South West Coast Path: 630 miles Minehead to Poole www.swcp.org.uk
Tarka Trail: 180 miles figure of eight route from Barnstaple
Templer Way: 18 miles, Haytor to Teignmouth
Two Castles Trail: 24 miles, Okehampton and Launceston
Two Moors Way: 102 miles Lynmouth to Ivybridge
West Devon Way: 36 miles Okehampton to Plymouth

Appendix E Pubs and Tearooms

Walk No	Place	Pub/Tearoom	Telephone No.
1	Countisbury,	Sandpiper Inn	01598 741358
1	Lynton,	Cliff Top Café	01598 753366
1	Watersmeet,	NT Tea Room	01598 753348
2	Brendon,	Rockford Inn	01598 741214
3	Heddons Valley,,	Hunters Inn	01598 763230
3	Parracombe	Fox & Goose	01598 763621
4	Molland,	London Inn	01769 550269
5	Eggesford,	Lymington Arms	01837 83572
6	Chawleigh,	Royal Oak	01769 580427
6	Chulmleigh,	The Old Court House	01769 580045
7	Zeal Monachorum,	The Waie Inn	01363 82348
8	Bickleigh,	Fishermans Cott	01884 855237

8	Bickleigh,	Trout	01884 855596
9	Culmstock,	Culm Valley Inn	01884 840354
10	Kentisbeare,	Keepers Cottage Inn	01884 266247
10	Broadhembury,	Drewe Arms	01404 841267
11	Stockland,	Kings Arms Inn	01404 881361
12, 13	Beer,	Anchor Inn	01297 20386
12	Colyton,	Gerrard Arms	01297 552588
13	Beer,	Anchor Inn	01297 20386
13	Branscombe,	Masons Arms	01297 680300
14	Tipton, St John	Golden Lion	01404 812881
15	Otterton,	Kings Arms Inn	01395 568416
15	Otterton,	Otterton Mill	01395 567041
17	Lustleigh,	The Cleave	01647 277223
17	Lustleigh,	Primrose Cottage	01647 277365
18	Bridford,	Bridford Inn	01647 252436
19	Belstone,	The Tors	01837 840689
22	Ilsington,	Carpenters Arms	01364 661215
23	Maidencombe,	Thatched Tavern	0870 2312672
24	Marldon,	Church House Inn	01803 558279
24	Compton Castle,	Barton Restaurant	01803 873314
24	Berry Pomeroy,	Castle Tearoom	01803 866618
25	Greenway,	National Trust	01803 661903
26	Coleton Fishacre	National Trust	01803 752466
28	East Prawle,	Pigs Nose	01548 511209
30	Hope Cove,	Hope & Anchor Inn	01548 561294
30	Bolberry,	Port Light Rest. & Inn	01548 561384
31	Burgh Island,	Pilchard Inn	01548 810514
31	Kingston,	Dolphin Inn	01548 810314
31	Ringmore,	Journey's End Inn	01548 810205
32	Noss Mayo,	Ship Inn	01752 872387
32	Noss Mayo,	Swan Inn	01752 872392
34	Milton Combe,	Who'd Have Thought It	01822 853313
34	Buckland Monachorum,	Drake Manor Inn	01822 853892
35	Roadford,	Roadford Lake	01566 784859
36	Sheepwash,	Half Moon Inn	01409 231376
37	Hartland Quay,	Hartland Quay Hotel	01237 441218
37	Docton,	Docton Mill	01237 441369
38	Parkham,	Bell Inn	08717 144568
38	Horns Cross,	Coach & Horses	01237 451214
39	Saunton,	Saunton Sands Hotel	01271 890212
40	Lee,	Grampus Inn	01271862906

Walk! UK series of guidebooks

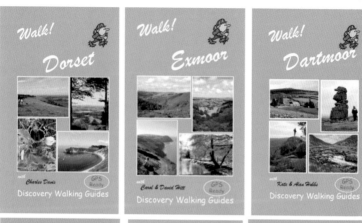

Discovery Walking Guides Ltd. 10 Tennyson Close. Northampton NN5 7HJ.
www.walking.demon.co.uk & www.dwgwalking.co.uk